Vocabulary

for TOEFL® iBT

NEW YORK

Library of Congress Cataloging-in-Publication Data:
Vocabulary for TOEFL iBT.
    p. cm.
    ISBN: 978-1-57685-632-1
    1. Test of English as a Foreign Language—Study guides. 2. English language—
Examinations—Study guides. 3. Vocabulary—Examinations—Study guides. 4.
English language—Ability testing. I. LearningExpress (Organization)
    PE1128.V63 2007
    428.0076—dc22

                                                                    2007026015

Printed in the United States of America

9 8 7 6 5 4 3 2 1

ISBN: 978-1-57685-632-1

For information on LearningExpress, other LearningExpress products, or bulk sales,
please write to us at:
    LearningExpress
    55 Broadway
    8th Floor
    New York, NY 10006

Or visit us at:
    www.learnatest.com

CONTENTS

Introduction

Everyone has three vocabularies in every language he or she speaks: a **reading vocabulary**, a **listening vocabulary**, and a **speaking vocabulary**. You've read words you have never heard, and heard words you've never read. Your speaking vocabulary may ignore many words you have either read or heard but do not use. As you explore the vocabulary in this book, think about bringing these three large sets of words together into a rich and useful database that will serve you well.

Discovering words you don't know may send your anxiety level soaring, and nobody does their best work when they're anxious. With practice, though, you can learn to take unknown words in stride. Here's how to start.

1. Start small. Don't tackle the whole sentence at once. There are several techniques for breaking sentences into smaller units. One way you can do this is to find a **verb** (an action word that tells you what's happening) and gradually incorporate the words around it into an increasingly longer phrase as you decipher its meaning. The verb provides an anchor for the meaning because it tells you what is being done.

    You can also use trial and error to find islands of meaning in a sentence. Find a word or a phrase you understand and start adding a word or two on either side. As you discover several such islands and gradually enlarge each one, you will eventually see how they fit together; and then you will understand the dynamics of the whole sentence.

2. If the vocabulary in a sentence is a problem, look at the words around it. Usually you can figure out what function a word is serving in the sentence. Ask yourself if it's an action word. If so, it's a verb. Is it describing something? Then it's an **adjective** or **adverb**. Is it the **subject**—the person, place or thing performing the action in the sentence? It's a **noun** or **pronoun**. Use the surrounding context to help you guess the meaning or at least the part of speech of an unfamiliar word.

3. As you are reading a sentence with blanks or with words you don't know, it can ease your anxiety to substitute words or sounds of your choosing in place of the unknown words. The words *something* and *whatever* work well

in many situations. You may find you prefer nonsense words instead. As the meaning of the sentence gradually becomes clear, you can start substituting words that might work in the sentence.

Obtaining a better vocabulary doesn't have to be hard work. It mostly takes curiosity. Remember those unfamiliar words you encounter in conversations or while reading. Take them apart. Welcome them to your world. Share them with your coworkers, friends, or family. You'll be greatly rewarded for your efforts—because long after you have finished this book and taken the TOEFL iBT, you'll still possess a wealthy vocabulary of English words!

HOW TO USE THIS BOOK

If you are trying to gain admission into universities where instruction is in English and this is not your native language, you will have to pass the TOEFL iBT (Test of English as a Foreign Language Internet-based test). The reason for this is simple: Academic institutions want to be sure that you can read, write, and comprehend spoken English so that you can succeed in the college classroom. Sometimes, this test will also be used to evaluate you by many government, licensing, and certification agencies, or exchange and scholarship programs.

Vocabulary for TOEFL iBT will help nonnative speakers build or renew vital vocabulary skills. Vocabulary is a broad topic, and it forms the foundation for reading comprehension, grammar, and spelling. For the TOEFL iBT, you will not be allowed to use a dictionary, thesaurus, or other reference tool to help you with unfamiliar words. In general, the better your basic vocabulary skills are, the better you will do on the entire TOEFL iBT.

Whether your exam is months away or coming up in a few weeks, this book will help you prepare. Begin getting ready for the TOEFL iBT by creating a study plan for yourself. Determine how much time you have until the test day, and then decide how much time you can devote to studying each week. With *Vocabulary for TOEFL iBT*, we suggest that you choose a time each day to improve your vocabulary. Think about when would be the best time for you. It may be first thing in the morning, during your commute to work, or before you go to bed at night. Whenever the time is right, just make sure you do it regularly—at least five days a week for a month. Once you establish a study plan for yourself, you should stick as closely as you can to your plan. Always keep your end goal in mind. If you study hard the first time, chances are you will not have to take this exam again—ever!

Now, once you have set a study plan for yourself, look at the table of contents to see the types of vocabulary topics covered in this book. You may want to tackle the chapters in sequence, or you may decide to study the sections that give you the most difficulty early on in your test preparation.

Each chapter is filled with practice questions to test the new skill you just read about. As you work through the practice questions, you may want to have a dictionary or thesaurus handy. This can help expand your bank of vocabulary words. After you answer the practice questions, you will undoubtedly want to check your answers against the answer explanation section at the end of each chapter.

Vocabulary for TOEFL iBT contains two practice tests at the end of the book. These tests will give you the chance to measure what you have learned and review any problem areas that you find. If after answering all the questions you feel like you need more practice, reread the questions and try responding one more time. Repetition is often the key to success and studies show that most repetitive tasks become part of a person's inventory of skills over time.

The book finishes with a helpful word list of more than 650 commonly tested vocabulary words (Appendix A). It will be very beneficial for you to add these words to your current vocabulary. We advise tackling the words on the list as you move through *Vocabulary for TOEFL iBT*, not waiting until the end of the book. Another helpful list—entitled Prefixes, Suffixes, and Word Roots—is included in Appendix B. Understanding the parts that make up a word can give you a clue about a word's definition, and this can help you make educated guesses when taking the TOEFL iBT.

About TOEFL iBT

The Test of English as a Foreign Language (TOEFL) is used to measure your ability to use English in an academic setting. The TOEFL is designed to indicate your ability to communicate by measuring the impact of reading, listening, speaking, and writing on effective communication. Strong ability in each of these four areas will be necessary as you continue learning in English.

WHO SHOULD TAKE THE TEST

Proficiency in English is essential if you are to follow class discussions and complete the reading and writing assignments in most college classes. In many courses, you may also be required to deliver oral presentations. And if you are applying to a graduate program, you may be given a position as a teaching assistant, which means you will be expected to help undergraduate students with their schoolwork, instruct them, and grade their assignments. In order to ensure that you can succeed even though you are not studying in your native language, and that you will be a competent teaching assistant if you are applying to graduate school, colleges and other institutions may require you to take the TOEFL. To determine if you need to take the TOEFL, you should contact each institution to which you are applying for admission.

OVERVIEW OF THE TEST

The entire TOEFL iBT will take approximately four hours to complete and all test sections will be completed in one day. The test is not computer-adaptive. In other words, each test taker receives the same range of questions. The test is worth a total of 120 points.

The first test section is Reading, followed by Listening, Speaking, and Writing. There will be a ten-minute break after the Listening section. After completing a section of the test, you will not be able to return to that section to finish or change your answers.

READING SECTION
(approximately 60–100 minutes) 30 total points
This section contains 3–5 reading passages, each followed by 12–14 questions.

Question Types	Language Skills Used	Topics	Source for Response
Factual information • 3–6 per set • 4 answer choices each • worth 1 point each	Reading	Identify information from text	Reading passage
Negative factual information • 2 per set at most • 4 answer choices each • worth 1 point each	Reading	Identify information in the text that is not true	Reading passage
Inference • 2 per set at most • 4 answer choices each • worth 1 point each	Reading	Identify information that is strongly suggested but not stated	Reading passage
Rhetorical purpose • 2 per set at most • 4 answer choices each • worth 1 point each	Reading	Identify why author makes a statement	Reading passage
Vocabulary • 3–5 per set • 4 answer choices each • worth 1 point each	Reading	Identify the meaning of a word in the text	Reading passage

Question Types	Language Skills Used	Topics	Source for Response
Reference • 2 per set at most • 4 answer choices each • worth 1 point each	Reading	Identify the grammatical relationship between two words in the text	Reading passage
Sentence simplification • 1 per set at most • 4 answer choices each • worth 1 point each	Reading	Identify the choice that restates the sentence indicated	Reading passage
Insert text • 1 per set at most • 4 answer choices each • worth 1 point each	Reading	Insert a sentence in the most appropriate place in a passage	Reading passage
Prose summary • 1 per set at most • 6 answer choices each • worth 2 points each	Reading	Choose the three most important ideas in the passage	Reading passage
Fill in a table • 1 per set at most • multiple answer choices • worth 3–4 points each	Reading	Complete a table organizing the main ideas	Reading passage

As you begin the Reading section of the TOEFL iBT, a passage will appear on the computer screen. A scrollbar on the right side of the screen will allow you to move to the end of a passage.

At the top of the computer screen is a navigational toolbar. (You should note that your time does not stop when you are using the toolbar feature.) The heading on the left of the toolbar will state the section of the test on which you are working: Reading. The center of the toolbar will state the question you are working on as well as the number of questions in the section. On the right will be a clock, indicating your remaining time. You may choose to hide the clock by clicking the Hide Time button located next to the clock. Above the clock function are six navigation buttons. Clicking on the View Text button will let you view the entire passage when answering questions. The Review button will allow you to review the questions that you have answered and make changes. You can adjust the volume by clicking the Volume button. A Help button will provide some additional assistance for you.

Finally, there are Back and Next buttons, which allow you to move back and forth between questions.

LISTENING SECTION
(approximately 60–90 minutes) 30 total points

Stimulus	Language Skills Used	Topics	Source for Response
4–6 lectures, each followed by 6 questions	Listening	Arts, life sciences, physical sciences, and social science	Details from lecture
2–3 conversations, each followed by 5 questions	Listening	Nonacademic situation on campus	Details from conversation

For the Listening section of the TOEFL iBT, you will listen to the lectures and conversations through a headset. An image depicting the lecture or conversation will appear on the screen. This picture is designed to help you imagine the situation. Difficult words or phrases in the passage may be defined for you. When the listening passage is complete, a question will appear on the screen.

A toolbar will appear at the top of the screen. The heading on the left of the toolbar will state the section of the test on which you are working: Listening. Like the toolbar for the Reading section, the Listening section toolbar will state which question you are working on, the number of questions in the section, and your remaining time. You may choose to use the Hide Time button located to the left of the clock. Above the clock are four navigation buttons. There is a Volume button that allows you to adjust the volume, a Help button that will provide some additional assistance, and a Next button that allows you to move to the next question. After selecting Next, you are asked to click the OK button to confirm that you want to move to the next question. In the Listening section, you may not go back and review questions.

SPEAKING SECTION
(approximately 20 minutes) 30 total points

Tasks	Language Skills Used	Topics	Source for Response	Preparation Time	Response Time
Task 1 (independent)	Speaking	Familiar things	Opinion	15 seconds	45 seconds
Task 2 (independent)	Speaking	Choose a side	Opinion	15 seconds	45 seconds

Tasks	Language Skills Used	Topics	Source for Response	Preparation Time	Response Time
Task 3 (integrated)	Reading, Listening, and Speaking	Nonacademic situation on campus	Details from materials given	30 seconds	60 seconds
Task 4 (integrated)	Reading, Listening, and Speaking	Academic topic	Details from materials given	30 seconds	60 seconds
Task 5 (integrated)	Listening and Speaking	School-related problem with two possible solutions	Opinion about materials given	20 seconds	60 seconds
Task 6 (integrated)	Listening and Speaking	Academic topic	Details from materials given	20 seconds	60 seconds

To take the Speaking section of the TOEFL iBT, you will be required to wear a headset with a microphone. For four of the speaking tasks, you will listen to the spoken materials through a headset. An image depicting the lecture or conversation will appear on the screen. For all of the speaking tasks, you will speak into the microphone to record your responses, which will be digitally recorded and sent to the ETS Online Scoring Network.

WRITING SECTION
(approximately 50 minutes) 30 total points

Tasks	Language Skills Used	Topics	Source for Response	Response Time
Task 1 (integrated)	Reading, Listening, and Writing	Academic topic	Details from materials given	20 minutes
Task 2 (independent)	Writing	Choose a side	Opinion	30 minutes

For the Writing section of the TOEFL iBT, you will type your response to two tasks. For the integrated writing task, you will listen to the spoken materials through a headset. Human raters rate writing responses through the ETS Online Scoring Network.

REGISTRATION

Because test centers fill up quickly, you should begin the TOEFL registration process right away.

HERE'S A HINT
THE INFORMATION AND REGISTRATION BULLETIN

Before you register for the TOEFL, you should obtain the *Information and Registration Bulletin*. The ETS created this document to provide you with all the important information you will need to know before you take the TOEFL iBT. It includes a list of test sites in all countries; institution codes, which you will need to report your scores to the colleges and universities you would like to attend; and other information you will find useful, such as sample questions, test instructions, and a list of writing topics. Request a bulletin as soon as possible if you have not already done so. You can pick up or request a bulletin:

- from admissions or international student offices at most colleges and universities
- from ETS representative offices
- from the TOEFL website, www.toefl.org
- by calling the ETS at 1-609-771-7100

You can register online at the TOEFL website, 24 hours a day, seven days a week. After completing the registration form, you will receive an instant e-mail confirmation. Payment methods include a valid credit card or an electronic check (if you have a bank account in the United States or its territories).

To register by phone, you must call at least seven days before the test date and pay using a valid credit card. You will be given a test date, reporting time, test center address, and a registration number, which you must bring to the test center on test day. To schedule a test date in the United States, Canada, or U.S. territories, call 1-800-GO-TOEFL (1-800-468-6335). If you live outside the United States and want to test in the United States, call 1-443-751-4862. To schedule a test date elsewhere, call the Regional Registration Center (RRC) for your area or country. A list of RRCs is printed in the *Information and Registration Bulletin*.

To register by mail, fill out the registration form in the *Information and Registration Bulletin*. You should receive a registration confirmation. If you do not, you must call the location where you mailed your registration at least three full business days before the registration deadline for your earliest test choice. To schedule a test date in the United States, Canada, or U.S. territories, mail your completed registration form and payment to the ETS at the following address:

ETS-TOEFL iBT Registration Office
P.O. Box 6152
Princeton, NJ 08541–6152, USA

To schedule a test date elsewhere, call the RRC for your area or country.

Although the ETS makes it possible to register by mail, online and phone registrations are quicker processes. Online and phone registrations must be completed one week before the test, while mailed registrations must be received at least four weeks before the test.

OFFICIAL SCORE REPORTS

At no cost, you can get one examinee score report and up to four official score reports sent to the institutions of your choice. You may choose those institutions up until 10 P.M. (local test center time) on the day prior to your test date. Fifteen days after you take the test, the examinee score report will be sent to you and official score reports will be sent to your selected institutions. The printed score report that is mailed to you will contain all of the final section scores as well as your total score.

You can have official score reports sent to institutions other than those you indicate when you register. Requests must be made online, by mail, or by fax. Reports requested online are mailed about four working days after your request. Reports requested by mail or fax are mailed about two weeks after receipt of your request. The cost is $17 for each report ordered.

Fifteen business days after completing your TOEFL iBT, you may view your scores online. TOEFL test scores are kept on file for two years after the test date. Scores more than two years old can't be reported.

HOW MUCH DOES THE TOEFL IBT COST?

The fee for the TOEFL iBT is $140. This includes an examinee score report and four score reports sent to institutions that you designate when you register for the test.

CANCELING OR RESCHEDULING YOUR EXAM

If your schedule changes and you can't make it to the test you have registered for, you can either reschedule or cancel your test date. If you reschedule, you will be

charged a $40 rescheduling fee. If you call to cancel at least three business days before your appointment, you will receive a refund of $65. In the United States, Canada, or U.S. territories, call 1-800-468-6335 to cancel or reschedule. For testing elsewhere, contact your RRC.

HOW THE TOEFL IBT IS SCORED

You will earn between 0 and 30 points for each of the four test areas. Your total score is calculated by adding the four skill area scores together. So, the total score will range from 0 to 120.

The Reading and Listening sections of the test consist of objective test items, meaning each question has a correct answer(s). The Speaking and Writing sections are subjective. This means that there is not one correct answer to these questions. Each of the six speaking tasks is awarded between 0 and 4 points based on a rubric. Each of the two writing tasks is awarded between 0 and 5 points based on a rubric. For each test section, the points are converted to a 0- to 30-point scale. All tasks are graded by trained human raters.

PASSING THE TOEFL

There is no single passing score on the TOEFL iBT. The institutions to which you are applying determine the minimum acceptable score. However, some colleges provide ESOL (English as a Second or Other Language) classes. If you score below what is required by the institution of your choice, you may be able to register for ESOL classes your first semester and continue on to other classes when you successfully complete the ESOL course. Alternatively, you can take the TOEFL iBT again. But one of the goals of this book is to prepare you to do your best and succeed the first time around.

CANCELING AND REINSTATING YOUR SCORES

If, after taking the exam, you feel that you didn't perform to the best of your ability and that your score is not high enough to get you into the program of your choice, you can cancel your score at the test center. If you do cancel your scores, they will not be reported to you or any institutions, and you will not receive a refund. After canceling your scores, you will be able to reinstate them provided that your request is received within ten days of your test date.

You may reinstate your scores by:

Phone
1-877-863-3546 (United States, Canada,
   and U.S. Territories)
1-609-771-7100 (all other locations)

Fax
1-609-771-7500

Mail
TOEFL Services
Educational Testing Service
P.O. Box 6151
Princeton, NJ 08541-6151 USA

Your request should include your name, date of birth, daytime phone number, registration number, and payment of the $20 reinstatement fee. The reinstatement will take approximately two weeks to be reported online, and the score report will be mailed shortly thereafter.

WRITING AND SPEAKING RESCORING

If you disagree with your score on the Writing and Speaking sections, you can request that your answers be rescored up to three months after your test date. You will be charged $60 for a Writing or a Speaking section rescore by scoring specialists. Complete the TOEFL iBT Rescoring Request Form, which is found on the TOEFL website. Rescoring results will be available about three weeks after the receipt of your rescoring request.

If the rescoring confirms your original score, you will be notified via mail. If there is a change in your score, you will receive a revised examinee score report. The institutions that you selected as score recipients will receive new official score reports. These revised scores will become your official scores.

ON TEST DAY

The ETS is very strict about identification for TOEFL test takers. If you fail to provide proper registration and identification documents on the day of the test, you will most likely not be admitted to the test center. To make sure your hard work and studying don't go to waste because you forgot a piece of paper, collect all the items you are taking to the test in advance and put them in a safe place. Read the identification requirements in the *Information and Registration Bulletin.* In most cases, a passport that has your photograph and signature will do. Your identification will be checked before you are admitted. You will also need your registration number.

TOEFL TEST CENTER PROCEDURES AND REGULATIONS

On the day of your exam, arrive at the test center at least 30 minutes early to allow time for registration and identification.

Before the test session, you will be required to write your signature and sign a confidentiality statement. Your picture will be taken and reproduced on your score report and the computer monitor you are using. If, for some reason, you have to leave your seat at any time other than the break, raise your hand. Timing of the section will not stop during an unscheduled break.

To receive an official score report, you must answer at least one question in each section. If, at any time during the test, you believe you have a problem with your computer or need the administrator for any reason, raise your hand. All testing sessions are subject to videotaping.

AGAINST THE RULES

Here is a list of things you are not allowed to do during the exam or exam breaks. Failure to comply with these rules may result in your dismissal from the test center and canceling of your scores without a refund.

DON'T:

- bring cellular phones, beepers, pagers, watch alarms, or electronic or photographic devices of any kind to the test session.
- eat, drink, smoke, or chew gum, except as permitted in designated areas of the testing center during breaks.

- refer to or use any testing materials or aids at any time during the testing session or break. The following are considered testing aids: pencils or pens, dictionaries, calculators, watch calculators, books, pamphlets, rulers, highlighter pens, translators, notes, or any other electronic or photographic devices or keyboards.
- leave the test center during the test session and break.
- exceed the time permitted for the break.
- attempt to take the test for someone else or fail to provide acceptable identification.
- create a disturbance or behave inappropriately.
- give or receive unauthorized help.
- attempt to tamper with the computer.
- attempt to remove test questions (in any format) from the testing room.

Follow these guidelines, and be sure to comply with the test administrator's directions at all times.

Vocabulary in Context

One of the most fundamental vocabulary skills is how to use context to determine meaning. Using a dictionary is, of course, the best way to define a word. But if you're in a testing situation and you are not allowed to use one, you must rely on the context clues in the sentence.

DEFINITION

context: the words and sentences that surround a word or phrase and help convey its meaning

Ever since you learned your first English words, you have been determining meaning from context. **Context** refers to the words and sentences that surround a particular word and help convey its meaning.

You can use the context of a sentence—or **context clues**—to help you detect the meaning of a word. Simply put, this means that you can look for clues in and around the vocabulary word. The term *context clues* means that other words in the sentence "give away" or "give clues" to the definition. For example, sometimes you'll find **synonyms** (words that mean the same thing) or **antonyms** (words that mean the opposite), or details that lead you to identify the vocabulary word in question. Once in a while, you'll find a group of words set off by commas (called an **appositive**), which gives you a very clear definition of the word.

HERE'S A HINT
USE IT OR LOSE IT

There's really only one rule for building your vocabulary: *Use it or lose it.* When you are learning a new word, if you don't use it, you will soon forget what it means. Write new words down on a vocabulary list. Use them in e-mails or letters to friends. Introduce them to members of your family. Use the words you learn in your everyday communications as much as possible so they become a permanent part of your vocabulary.

Now, notice how the context of the sentence below helps give the word *candor* its meaning:

➡ I admire Arun's <u>candor</u>, but sometimes, he can be a bit *too* honest.
   Candor means
   a. irritability.
   b. frank, sincere speech.
   c. readiness to judge or criticize others.
   d. comfort with speaking in front of people.

Based on the context of the sentence, only **b** can be the correct answer. The speaker tells you that Arun is sometimes *too* honest, thus signifying that *candor* means frank, sincere speech—Arun tells people exactly what he thinks.

Even if you can't figure out exactly what *candor* means, you can tell from the context whether it is something positive or negative, and this can help you narrow down your answer choices on an exam. In this case, because the speaker admires Arun's candor, you can assume that candor is a positive thing. You can therefore eliminate choices **a** and **c**.

There a four types of context clues that can help you:

1. Restatement
2. Positive/Negative
3. Contrast
4. Specific Detail

This sentence uses two types of context clues: restatement and positive/negative. The first part of the sentence tells you that candor is a good thing (positive/negative),

while the second part essentially restates the meaning of the word. Here's another example of a sentence that uses these two types of context clues:

➡ Hani suddenly found himself *destitute*, so poor that he could barely afford to eat.

The context clearly reveals that *destitute* is not a positive word; it is not a good thing to be so poor one can barely afford to eat. The context also restates the meaning of *destitute*, essentially defining the word within the sentence, so that you can tell exactly what *destitute* means—extremely poor.

There are two other types of context clues to watch for. Read the following paragraph as an example (but *don't* look up the italicized words!):

> Sarah had worked so hard for the past few weeks that she decided she owed herself a day of complete *indolence*. Saturday, she slept until noon, ordered take-out so she wouldn't have to cook, and left the dishes in the sink. She left her chores for another day and spent the afternoon lying on the couch, reading and watching television. But on Sunday, she was back to her old *assiduous* self, and by noon, she had already cleaned her whole apartment, done her grocery shopping, and paid her bills.

How do you know what *indolence* means? From two more types of context clues: contrast and specific detail. The first sentence suggests that *indolence* is in contrast to working hard, while the second and third sentences confirm this with specific details. Thus you can determine what *indolence* means. Let's say you were given the choices below:

  a. luxurious
  b. hard labor
  c. deep sleep
  d. laziness

The correct answer is **d**, laziness. The specific details tell you that Sarah did her best to laze around the house all day. Besides, you know the other answers are incorrect because Sarah didn't do anything luxurious (choice **a**) and she didn't do any work or chores (choice **b**). There's no mention of sleep in the paragraph, so choice **c** is also incorrect.

Now let's look at the context in which *assiduous* is used. Again, you have two kinds of context clues: contrast and specific detail. You know that the *assiduous* Sarah of

Sunday was very different from the *indolent* Sarah of Saturday (contrast). You also know what the *assiduous* Sarah does: She is very, very busy on Sunday, cleaning and working around the house (specific detail). *Assiduous* means diligent, hardworking; or persevering, unremitting.

DENOTATION AND CONNOTATION

The **denotation** of a word is simply its dictionary definition. For instance, look at the dictionary definitions of the following words.

- ➡ procrastination: to postpone or delay needlessly
- ➡ lazy: to be resistant to work or exertion; slow moving or sluggish
- ➡ inactive: not active or not tending to be active; not functioning or operating

Some English words, however, have more than one meaning. A *quack*, for example, is the sound a duck makes, but a *quack* is also an untrained or unqualified person who pretends to be a doctor.

Words also have another meaning beyond their denotation. Each word also has a **connotation**—an implied meaning or emotional impact. Sometimes, the connotation can be favorable or positive. Other times the connotation can be unfavorable or negative. Then again, some words do not arouse any emotion at all and have a neutral connotation.

For example, if you were to look up the word *playful* in the dictionary, you might get a definition similar to that of two of its synonyms, *spirited* and *mischievous*. But all three of these words have different connotations and bring to mind different feelings. *Spirited* has a positive connotation and *mischievous* a negative connotation, while *playful* is neutral in tone.

DEFINITIONS

denotation: a word's exact meaning or dictionary definition

connotation: a word's implied meaning or emotional impact

When you come across an unfamiliar word, the context will often reveal a great deal about the connotation of that word, even if it does not provide enough information for you to determine its denotation. At a minimum, the connotations of the surrounding words will usually tell you whether the vocabulary word is positive or negative. Therefore, when you are looking for context clues, make sure you look at the surrounding words carefully and consider their denotations and connotations.

HERE'S A HINT
ALL SYNONYMS ARE NOT CREATED EQUAL

Synonyms are words that share the same meaning or nearly the same meaning as other words. It is important to know that there are often many synonyms for one word. While some synonyms can be similar, they are rarely identical. For instance, the words *bountiful, ample, plentiful,* and *glut* suggest abundance. However, one of these words suggests an overabundance. While you can have a bountiful, ample, or plentiful supply of food on the table for a dinner party, a glut of food is an excessive amount of food that suggests there will be waste involved. It is important to choose your words carefully and to be as clear as possible when choosing synonyms.

Although some synonyms are interchangeable, most words have their own unique connotation. So while test questions will often ask you to identify synonyms such as *laconic, terse,* and *succinct,* when it comes to your own communications, you should choose your words carefully. *Terse,* for example, has the most positive connotation of these three words, suggesting brevity with a sense of polish or elegance. *Succinct* is more neutral, conveying a sense of compactness or tightness in how an idea has been expressed. *Laconic,* on the other hand, conveys the same basic idea but with the suggestion of brusqueness or abruptness. Thus, although these words are effectively synonymous, each word carries its own specific connotation and leaves a slightly different impression.

HOW MUCH CONTEXT DO YOU NEED?

In the passage about Sarah, you would still be able to understand the main idea of the passage even if you did not know—or could not figure out—the meanings of *indolence* and *assiduous.* In some cases, though, your understanding of a sentence or paragraph depends on your understanding of a particular word or phrase. For example, you can't understand what *inept* means from the following example sentence—it simply does not provide sufficient context. In fact, you can't even figure out if it is something positive or negative, because the sentence provides almost no context at all:

➡   Sabina is an utterly *inept* dancer.

Is Sabina a *graceful* dancer? An *awkward* dancer? Or an *accomplished* dancer? You simply cannot tell from the context. But you *could* figure out what *inept* means by breaking down the word into its prefix (*in-*) and word root (*ept*). That's the subject of Chapters 2 and 3. Meanwhile, however, here's a sentence that does give you the context you need to determine the meaning of the word:

➡ Despite years of lessons, Sabina remains an utterly *inept* dancer who simply stumbles across the dance floor.

Now we can tell through context that *inept* means *awkward* or *clumsy*. Being able to determine the meaning of unfamiliar words from their context is an essential vocabulary skill. Sometimes you will find unfamiliar words whose meanings are indecipherable without a dictionary. More often than not, though, a careful look at the context will give you enough clues to interpret the definition.

By looking for the way the words are used in the paragraph, you can figure out what these words mean. Even if you have no idea what a word means, you can still tell something about the word by how it is used—by examining the words and ideas surrounding it. Like detectives looking for clues at a crime scene, you must look at the passage for clues that will uncover the definition of the word.

SENTENCE DETECTIVE

Deciphering some sentences can seem like an impossible mission, but like everything else worth doing, it's hard at first and gets easier as you practice. There are some basic skills you need to acquire, though. Think of yourself as a detective trying to decode a secret message. Once you have the key to the code, it's easy to decipher the message. The following sections will give you the keys you need to unlock the meanings of even the most complex sentences. The great thing is that these are master keys that can unlock any and all sentences, including the many complex sentences you will encounter in your college reading.

▶ *Sentence Structure*

The single most important key to the meaning of a sentence is its structure. The best and easiest way to determine sentence structure is to look at its punctuation.

Sentence completion questions always have one or more commas or semicolons. The basic strategy is to separate the sentence into units divided by punctuation. Often, one of the units will express a complete thought, then at least one unit will have one or two blanks. The unit that expresses a complete thought will tell you what the unit(s) with blank(s) need to say. For example, consider this sample question:

Select the word that best fills in the blank.

➡ After finding sacred objects inside numerous Mayan caves, archaeologists have begun to revise their opinion that the Maya used the caves solely for _____ functions.
   a. reverent
   b. theological
   c. religious
   d. secular

When you divide this sentence into punctuation-defined units, you have:

After finding sacred objects inside numerous Mayan caves,

   and

archaeologists have begun to revise their opinion that the Maya used the caves solely for _____ functions.

The first unit, the unit without the blank, tells you that the second unit has something to do with what happened 1) *after* finding sacred objects and 2) in Mayan caves. The second unit, the one with the blank, tells you that 1) archaeologists have begun to revise their opinion and 2) their opinion (before being revised) was that Mayan caves were used only (*solely*) for some kind of function. Your mission is to figure out what goes in the blank, namely what kind of function archaeologists used to think the caves were exclusively used for.

Now you're ready to use the first unit to illuminate the second. If scientists used to think *one thing* until they found *sacred objects*, it means they used to think the caves were *not* used for sacred purposes. Now you know you need to fill in the blank with a word that means "not sacred," a word such as *civic*, or *secular*. Your final step is to look at the answer choices to find the one that matches the idea you have formed about what needs to be in the blank(s). Choice **d**, *secular*, is the best answer choice.

Here's an example of a sample question that doesn't divide neatly into a complete unit and an incomplete unit. This question has a blank in each of its two units.

Select the words that best fill in the blanks:

➡ The famous daredevil was actually quite _____ by temperament, as illustrated by the fact that he did not _____ until he was two years old.
   a. reckless . . . amble
   b. careful . . perambulate
   c. adventurous . . . rest
   d. daring . . . scuttle

The first unit is *The famous daredevil was actually quite _____ by temperament.* The word *actually* tells us that there is something unexpected going on. If *actually* were to be removed from the sentence, there'd be no way you could know what kind of words go in the blanks. *Actually* is a clue word, one that points you toward the meaning of the sentence. The *famous daredevil actually* had an unexpected kind of temperament. What kind of temperament would you expect a famous daredevil to have? Adventurous, bold, daring, right? So the word that goes in the first blank will be one that has a contrasting relationship to that expected temperament.

The second unit of the sentence, *as illustrated by the fact that he did not _____ until he was two years old*, uses a phrase of comparison, *as illustrated by*, to let us know that the word that goes in the blank should complete the idea of the daredevil's having a temperament that is not bold. Think of a synonym for "not bold." Put it in the first blank. Now read the sentence using your word in the first blank. Think of something that, if not done before age two, would indicate that kind of temperament. The next thing you do is look at the answer choices for words that are similar to the ones you chose. The best answer to this question is choice **b**, *careful . . . perambulate*. Even if you didn't know that to *perambulate* is to walk, or move about on one's own, you could be fairly confident that you had the right answer because *careful* is such a good choice.

▶ *A Clue for You*

The second important skill you must master for sentence completion questions is the ability to identify key words and phrases. These are the words that most help you decode the sentence. Think of them as clues to a mystery. Among the most useful of these are the words that enable you to identify the logical relationship between the complete unit(s) of the sentence and the incomplete unit(s). As in the preceding example, sometimes you have to complete one portion of a two-blank sentence before you can work on the logical relationship of another unit.

There are three types of logical relationships commonly expressed in sentence completion questions: contrast, comparison, and cause and effect. Mastering these three relationships will help you succeed on sentence completion questions.

CONTRAST

Some words that logically signal a relationship of contrast are: *though, although, however, despite, but,* and *yet.* Can you think of others? There are also phrases that signal a contrast between the units of the sentence, such as *on the other hand, but, however, despite,* or *on the contrary.*

Try making a sentence using these words and phrases. See how the two parts of your sentence oppose each other. This is the logical relationship of contrast, or opposition. No matter how complex a sentence completion question seems at first glance, when you see one of these words or phrases, you will know you're looking at a sentence that expresses one thought in its complete unit and a contrasting thought in the incomplete unit. First you decipher the thought in the complete unit, then fill in the blank in the incomplete unit with a word that expresses a contrasting thought. For example:

➡ Although the tiger is primarily a solitary beast, its cousin the lion is a
_____ animal.

First divide the sentence into two units, using the punctuation to guide you. Now you have as the first unit, *Although the tiger is primarily a solitary beast,* and, *its cousin the lion is a _____ animal,* as the second unit. The first unit tells you by the use of the word *although* that the second unit will express a relationship of opposition or contrast. You can see that tigers and lions are being contrasted. The word that goes in the blank has to be an adjective that describes *animal* in the way that *solitary* describes *beast.* Therefore the word that will contrast with the idea in the first unit is in opposition to *solitary.* What is an antonym of *solitary*? Solitary means alone. You might choose the word *social. Friendly, gregarious,* or *sociable* are other options, all meaning "not solitary." Then you look for the word in the answer choices that is a synonym of the word you chose.

COMPARISON

There are two kinds of comparison relationships: comparison by similarity and comparison by restatement. Words that signal comparison include *likewise, similarly,* and *and.* Phrases that introduce comparisons are *just as, as well as, for example, as shown,* and *as illustrated by.* Words and phrases that precede restatement are *namely, in other words, in fact,* and *that is.* Relationships of logical comparison are straightforward. The idea expressed in the complete unit of the sentence is similar to or the same as the idea that needs to be expressed in the incomplete unit. When you know what the complete unit says, you know what the incomplete unit needs to say—the same thing, or very nearly so. Here's an example of a comparison sentence:

➡ Until he went to military school, Foster never stood up straight; as illustrated by his _____ in this photograph.

This sentence has three units, two complete and one incomplete. The first two units tell you that before military school, Foster slouched. The blank in the third unit, therefore, needs to be filled by a word that will illustrate his slouching. The correct answer will be *posture*, or its synonym.

ON YOUR OWN
PRACTICE REALLY LISTENING

Some of the best resources for nonnative English speakers trying to increase their vocabularies are CDs or audiotapes. English is a difficult language because it is so visually confusing. One of the ways you most often encounter vocabulary is by listening.

Vocabulary CDs and tapes are available in libraries and bookstores. You may also find it helpful to use a nonfiction or fiction book and the same book in audio form (CD or audiotape). Play the audio version of the book as you read along in the book. This will help you match the word to its written form.

CAUSE AND EFFECT

A third kind of logical relationship often expressed in sentence completion questions is the cause and effect relationship. In other words, the sentence states that one thing is a result of something else. Again, you can rely on key words to point you in the right direction. Words such as *thus, therefore, consequently,* and *because,* and phrases such as *due to, as a result,* and *leads to* signal a cause and effect relationship. Try making some cause and effect sentences to see how they work.

Here's an example of a cause and effect sample question.

Select the word that best fills in the blank.

➡ Scientific knowledge is usually _____, often resulting from years of hard work by numerous investigators.
a. cumulative
b. illogical
c. decreasing
d. irrelevant

The complete unit of the sentence, *often resulting from years of hard work by numerous investigators,* tells you that the other unit results from *numerous investigators* working *hard* for *years.* The incomplete unit, the one with the blank, tells you that you are looking for a word to describe *scientific knowledge* as a result of those years of hard work. You know that whatever word the test makers are looking for, it must have something to do with *lots of stuff,* because years of hard work by numerous investigators would produce a lot of something. The best answer choice for this question is choice **a,** *cumulative,* which, of course, applies to *lots of stuff.*

 ## HERE'S A HINT
MIX AND MATCH SENTENCES

To help you remember some important verbs and adjectives, match verbs and adjectives together in pairs that will help you recall their meaning. Here are several examples:

- You *abhor* what is *odious.*
- You might *disdain* something that is *banal.*
- You won't be *daunted* if you are *intrepid;* you will be *daunted* if you are *timid.*
- You might *tout* something about which you are *fervent.*
- You might *vacillate* if you are *timid* or *diffident.*
- You might *grovel* if you are *servile.*

You can also mix and match words to create synonym and antonym pairs. *Abate* and *ebb,* for example, have nearly the same meaning, while *disdain* and *revere* are opposites.

Once you learn how to identify the complete and incomplete units of a sentence using punctuation to guide you, you've made a good start. Next you determine the logical relationship of the units, using key words and phrases; and then you understand what the sentence is saying, even if there's some vocabulary you don't understand. But if you keep working on building your vocabulary, chances are you will understand the crucial words.

ACTIVE READING

As you might expect, vocabulary in context questions ask you to determine the meanings of particular words. To prepare for these types of questions on the

TOEFL iBT, it is a good idea to become an active reader. This is a skill you can practice every day. As you read an English-language newspaper or magazine, have a dictionary handy. Look up as many unfamiliar words as you can so that your bank of vocabulary words becomes as large as possible.

This may sound like a contradiction, but if you make a habit of taking the time to read carefully and actively, you will actually spend *less* time learning the meaning of new vocabulary words. By reading carefully, you will often be able to determine meaning from context. By reading actively, you will continually expand your bank of vocabulary words—and the bigger your word base, the more you will comprehend, and the less time you will spend looking up words.

TIPS AND STRATEGIES

Vocabulary-in-context questions are common on standardized tests, like the TOEFL iBT. Here are some specific tips and strategies to use while preparing for and taking the exam:

- On any vocabulary-in-context question on an exam, there *will* be some kind of context clue to help you determine meaning. Remember the four types: restatement, positive/negative, contrast, and specific detail.
- Remember that you have a very powerful tool on a multiple-choice exam: the process of elimination. From the start, you can usually eliminate one or two answers that you know are incorrect. For example, you can eliminate negative choices if the context suggests the word is positive.
- To help you eliminate answers, read the sentence with each answer choice substituted for the vocabulary word. Often, putting the word in the context of the sentence can help you determine whether an answer is right or wrong.
- Consider the tone and connotation of the other words in the sentence. At a minimum, this can often help you determine whether the vocabulary word is positive or negative.
- Look for introductory words and phrases such as *unfortunately, however, surprisingly*. These words often tell you whether the word is positive or negative and/or set up contrast clues.
- Read carefully. Look for specific details that provide clues to meaning.
- If you have heard the vocabulary word before but aren't sure what it means, try to remember the context in which you heard it used before. This may help you better use the context as it is presented on the exam.

PRACTICE QUESTIONS

Choose the best vocabulary word to fill the blank. Circle your choices or write your answers on a separate piece of paper. Then compare your selections to the correct answers at the end of the chapter.

1. The _____ president differs from the past president on healthcare reform issues.
   a. talkative
   b. accomplished
   c. artificial
   d. incumbent

2. The _____ data supports the belief that there has been an increase in population in the county.
   a. nominal
   b. demographic
   c. practical
   d. nocturnal

3. The _____ collected from real estate taxes helped to balance the town budget.
   a. domain
   b. remainder
   c. revenue
   d. assessment

4. She pretended to be _____ about the new job opportunity, but secretly she was very excited.
   a. dedicated
   b. receptive
   c. candid
   d. blasé

5. We were tired when we reached the _____, but the spectac..
   view of the valley below was worth the hike.
   a. circumference
   b. summit
   c. fulcrum
   d. nadir

6. The suit had a(n) _____ odor, as if it had been stored in a trunk for
   a long time.
   a. aged
   b. scented
   c. musty
   d. decrepit

7. Because his workplace was so busy and noisy, he longed most of all for
   _____.
   a. solitude
   b. association
   c. loneliness
   d. irrelevancy

8. The teacher put the crayons on the bottom shelf to make them
   _____ to the young children.
   a. accessible
   b. receptive
   c. eloquent
   d. ambiguous

9. My computer was state-of-the-art when I bought it three years ago, but
   now it is _____.
   a. current
   b. dedicated
   c. unnecessary
   d. outmoded

10. Visiting all the tea shops in the city, they were on a _____ to find the perfect cup of tea.

   a. surge

   b. quest

   c. discovery

   d. cadence

11. Make sure the directions are very *explicit* so that no one makes a mistake. *Explicit* means

   a. intricate, complex.

   b. clearly and fully stated.

   c. chronologically ordered.

   d. ambiguous or implied.

12. The hotel is *teeming* with security personnel because the leaders of several countries are here for a summit meeting. *Teem* means

   a. to close down temporarily.

   b. to lose business due to circumstances beyond one's control.

   c. to be full of, nearly overflowing.

   d. to be under close scrutiny.

13. Karen was relieved to learn that the chemicals in her well water were all *benign. Benign* means

   a. natural.

   b. dangerous.

   c. of local origin.

   d. harmless.

14. Although it was *futile* because he didn't meet half of the requirements, Jensen applied for the job anyway because it was his dream position. *Futile* means

   a. useless.

   b. fruitful.

   c. radical.

   d. insane.

15. The editor, preferring a more *terse* writing style, cut 500 words from the 2,000-word article. *Terse* means
   a. elegant.
   b. factual.
   c. descriptive.
   d. concise.

16. Victor Frankenstein spent the last years of his life chasing his *elusive* monster, who was always one step of his creator. *Elusive* means
   a. difficult to compare.
   b. difficult to capture.
   c. difficult to forget.
   d. difficult to avoid.

17. Xiu's timely joke served to *diffuse* the tension in the room, and the rest of the meeting was highly productive. *Diffuse* means
   a. to refuse.
   b. to intensify.
   c. to create.
   d. to soften.

18. I completely lost track of Tula's point because she kept *digressing* to unrelated topics. *Digress* means
   a. to deviate, stray.
   b. to regress, revert.
   c. to change the tone.
   d. to express concisely.

19. The senator *evaded* the question by changing the subject and accusing his opponent of misconduct. *Evade* means
   a. to escape or elude.
   b. to answer indirectly.
   c. to refuse to answer directly.
   d. to deceive.

20. Samantha hasn't said why she's been so withdrawn lately, but I would *surmise* that it is because she is still upset about not being able to go to camp. *Surmise* means
   a. to confirm.
   b. to surprise.
   c. to believe.
   d. to guess.

21. Their conversation was considered playful _____ between two old friends.
   a. antics
   b. banter
   c. behavior
   d. activities

22. He tried to _____ the sinking morale of his friend in the hospital.
   a. sustain
   b. foster
   c. bolster
   d. nourish

ANSWERS

How did you do on identifying context clues? Check your answers here, and then analyze the results to figure out your plan of attack for mastering this topic.

1. **d.** *Incumbent* means holding any post or position.
2. **b.** *Demographic* data is the branch of research that deals with human populations.
3. **c.** *Revenue* is the income of a government.
4. **d.** *Blasé* means bored or unimpressed by things after having seen or experienced them too often.
5. **b.** The *summit* means the highest point, where the hikers would have a good view.
6. **c.** A *musty* odor is one that is stale or moldy.
7. **a.** *Solitude*, unlike loneliness, can be a desirable thing, and it would be something a person who works in a busy office would crave.
8. **a.** *Accessible* means capable of being reached or being within easy reach.

9. **d.** *Outmoded* means no longer in style or no longer usable.

10. **b.** A *quest* is a search or pursuit of something, in this case for the perfect cup of tea.

11. **b.** *Explicit* means clearly and fully stated; straightforward, exact. The context tells you that the directions need to be clear to prevent an error. If the directions are clearly and fully stated, it will help ensure that no one makes a mistake.

12. **c.** To *teem* means to be full of, to be present in large numbers. Numerous security personnel typically surround the leader of a country. If there is a meeting of several foreign leaders, there is likely to be a great number of security officers in the hotel.

13. **d.** *Benign* means not harmful or malignant; gentle, mild, having a beneficial effect. Choice **d** is the only answer that makes sense in the context of the sentence; Karen would logically be worried about chemicals in her water and relieved if she learned those chemicals were harmless.

14. **a.** *Futile* means useless, producing no result, hopeless, vain. Jensen's application is useless because he does not meet the minimum requirements for the job.

15. **d.** *Terse* means concise, using no unnecessary words. The main clue is that the editor cut the article by 25%, dramatically reducing its wordiness.

16. **b.** *Elusive* means evasive, eluding the grasp; difficult to capture. The sentence tells you that Dr. Frankenstein was never able to catch the creature, who constantly escaped his grasp.

17. **d.** To *diffuse* means to spread throughout, disperse; to soften or make less brilliant. Xiu's joke softened the tension so that the meeting could be more productive.

18. **a.** To *digress* means to turn aside, deviate; to stray from the main subject in writing or speaking. The speaker loses track of the point because Tula keeps shifting from the main topic to unrelated subjects.

19. **a.** To *evade* means to elude or avoid by cleverness or deceit; to avoid fulfilling, answering, or doing. The senator avoids answering the question by changing the subject.

20. **d.** To *surmise* means to form a notion from scanty evidence. The narrator is guessing that Samantha has been withdrawn because she is upset about not being able to go to camp.

21. **b.** *Banter* is defined as remarks or talk that is playful and teasing. Choice **a** is incorrect because antics are unpredictable behavior or actions. Choices **c** and **d** are incorrect because their definitions are too broad and do not focus on conversation.

22. **c.** If the friend has a "sinking morale," this means that the friend's feelings or attitude are overwhelmed or defeated. The speaker would, thus, want to raise or *bolster* this morale. Choice **a**, **b**, and **d** are all incorrect. The speaker would not want his friend's morale to continue to sink.

Using Prefixes and Suffixes

When you come across unfamiliar words without context, breaking those words into their parts can help you determine their meaning. This chapter reviews prefixes and suffixes and how you can use them to add new words to your vocabulary—and better understand words you already know.

A good knowledge of prefixes and suffixes is essential to building an effective vocabulary. The more familiar you are with these fundamental word parts, the easier it will be to determine the meaning of unfamiliar words.

There are dozens of prefixes and suffixes in the English language. Learning prefixes and suffixes in another language may seem like a daunting task, but the job may be easier than you think. Though prefixes and suffixes often appear in books like this with sophisticated vocabulary words, you are already using the same prefixes and suffixes with simple words that you already know well.

PREFIXES

Prefixes are syllables attached to the beginning of words to change or add to the meaning of the root word in some way. For example, the word *prefix* itself uses the prefix *pre-*, meaning before. Thus the meaning of the root word, *fix*, changes:

31

fix: to place securely or firmly

prefix: something placed at the beginning of a word

Several of the vocabulary words you studied in Chapter 2 used prefixes, including *inept*, which uses the prefix *in-*, meaning not—not suitable or competent.

ON YOUR OWN
IMMERSE YOURSELF IN WORDS

Get in the habit of noticing words all the time. Carry a small notebook with you and write down interesting words as you encounter them in your daily life. Don't know how to spell a word you hear? It doesn't matter—write it down just as it sounds to you and look it up later.

Knowledge of prefixes can help you in many ways as you build your vocabulary and as you prepare for the TOEFL iBT. Although you can't determine meaning based on a prefix alone—you also need to know the root of the word—you *can* often use a prefix to determine whether a word is positive or negative, to eliminate incorrect answers, and to provide partial context for the meaning of the word. For example, take the word *polyglot*. If you know that the prefix *poly-* means many, you can eliminate all but the correct answer in the following question:

➡ A *polyglot* is someone who
  a. is an expert in global issues.
  b. administers lie detector tests.
  c. is easily frightened.
  d. speaks many languages.

Choice **d** is the only answer that includes the idea of *many* or *multiple*. Thus, it is the only possible correct answer.

DEFINITIONS

root: the main part of a word; the base upon which prefixes and suffixes are added

prefix: syllable(s) attached to the beginning of a word to change or add to its meaning

suffix: syllable(s) attached to the end of a word to change or add to its meaning

You will not always be so lucky as to eliminate all of the incorrect answers, but even eliminating two or three will be a great help. For example, knowing that the

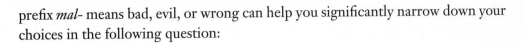

prefix *mal-* means bad, evil, or wrong can help you significantly narrow down your choices in the following question:

➡ To *malign* means
    a. to arrange.
    b. to speak badly about.
    c. to charm, enchant.
    d. to cast an evil spell.

With your knowledge of prefixes, you can eliminate choices **a** and **c**, leaving you with a 50–50 chance of choosing the correct answer. If you recall any context in which you have heard the word *malign* before, you may be able to choose the correct answer, **b**. To *malign* is to say evil, harmful, and often untrue things about someone; to speak ill of.

HERE'S A HINT
NUMERICAL PREFIXES

Probably among the most easily recognized of the prefixes are the numerical prefixes; that is, those that can tell something about the number represented by the word. Take a look at some words that contain numerical prefixes: *bipartisan* (two parties), *triage* (responding to the needs in order of priority, traditionally in three orders of priority), and *trilogy* (a series of three plays). Among the most common number related prefixes are:

    un-, mono-: one (unique, unity, monotonous, monopoly)
    bi-: two (bigamy, bilateral, bicameral, bicycle)
    tri-: three (trivial, trident, trinity, triple)
    quad-, quar-: four (quadrant, quarter, quart, quartet)
    deci-: ten (decade, decathlon, decimal, decibel)
    cent-: hundred (century, centipede, centennial)
    mil-: thousand (millipede, millennium, millimeter)

Following is a list of the prefixes. For each prefix, we have provided two examples of words that use that prefix. With a few exceptions, these examples are not test-prep words; rather, they are basic words that are probably already a part of your vocabulary. This will help you remember the meaning of each prefix—and show you just how well you already know them.

▶ *Common Prefixes*

a-, an-: not, without
amoral (not moral), *atypical* (not typical)

ab-, abs-: from, away, off
abduct (to take by force), *abnormal* (away from or apart from the standard)

ante-: prior to, in front of, before
anterior (placed before), *antedate* (to proceed in time, come before)

anti-, ant-: opposite, opposing, against
antibiotic (substance that kills microorganisms), *antidote* (remedy for counteracting the effects of a poison)

circ-, circum-: around, about, on all sides
circumference (the outer boundary of a circle), *circumstance* (the conditions or state of affairs surrounding or affecting an event, a particular incident, or an occurrence)

co-, com-, con-: with, together, jointly
cooperate (to work together, comply), *connect* (to bind or fasten together)

dis-: away from, apart, reversal, not
dismiss (to send away from, eject), *disobedient* (not obedient)

ex-: out, out of, away from
exit (go out), *expel* (to drive out or away)

in-: not
inaccurate (not accurate), *informal* (not formal)

inter-: between, among, within
intercept (to stop someone or something between its starting point and destination), *intervene* (to come, occur, appear, or lie between two points of time or things)

mal-: bad, abnormal, evil, wrong

malfunction (to fail to function properly), *malpractice* (wrongdoing, especially improper or negligent treatment of a patient by a physician)

mis-: bad, wrong, ill; opposite or lack of

misbehave (to behave badly), *misspell* (to spell incorrectly)

multi-: many, multiple

multimedia (the combined use of several media), *multiple* (having several or many parts or elements)

neo-: new, recent, a new form of

neonatal (of or relating to a newborn child), *neologism* (a new word or phrase)

non-: not

nonfiction (the genre of literature that includes all types of books other than fiction), *nonsmoker* (someone who does not smoke)

poly-: many, much

polygamy (the system of having more than one wife at a time), *polysyllabic* (having three or more syllables)

pre-: before

precaution (something done in advance to avoid risk), *predict* (to forecast, make known in advance)

re-: back, again

rebuild (to build again after destruction), *replace* (to put back in its former position; to take the place of)

sub-: under, beneath, below

subdue (to overcome, bring under control), *submarine* (a ship that can operate under water)

super-: above, over, exceeding

superb (grand, magnificent, of unusually high quality, excellent), *superman* (a man with powers exceeding ordinary human capacity)

A more comprehensive list of the most common English prefixes is located in Appendix B. After you have completed this chapter, make sure you review the list carefully and study any prefixes that are unfamiliar to you.

HERE'S A HINT
SOUNDS LIKE . . .

As you use your knowledge of prefixes and suffixes to determine meaning, see if you can recall hearing or using any words with similar roots or sounds. For example, you may realize that *agrarian* sounds like it shares a root word with *agriculture*—and it does. Even if you don't know exactly what *agriculture* means, you might know that it has something to do with land and its cultivation. You may also realize that the suffix *-ian* calls for an adjective, not a verb.

The point of learning about prefixes is to be able to notice how they can change word meanings in recognizable ways. Some prefixes immediately change the entire meaning of a word. For example, the prefixes *un-*, *in-*, *dis-*, and *il-* immediately signal that the word is the opposite of its root, as in *unhappy, inconsiderate, displeasing,* and *illegible.*

Other prefixes only remotely affect word meaning. For example, there is only a distant hint of the prefix *deci-*, which means "ten," in the word *decimate*, which means "to completely destroy." Historically, the word *decimate* meant to destroy a tenth of someone's property. Now we hardly recognize that meaning in the present definition.

The important point to remember is that in learning prefixes, you are not looking to memorize a long list of disconnected word parts, but to recognize familiar examples that you can apply to new words when you encounter them.

ON YOUR OWN
GO TO PLACES WHERE ENGLISH IS SPOKEN

The more you listen to English being spoken, the more you will understand. Visit a local park or museum where you will hear English around you. Go to the movie theater to see a film in English, or rent a film in your native language and watch it with English subtitles. Try watching the evening news. Listening well will improve your English vocabulary.

SUFFIXES

Suffixes are syllables added to the end of words to change or add to their meaning. They often change a word's part of speech, thereby also changing how the word functions in a sentence. Suffixes tell you whether a word is a person, place, or thing (a **noun**); an action or state of being (a **verb**); or a modifier, which is a word that describes (an **adjective** or **adverb**).

HERE'S A HINT
PARTS OF SPEECH

The following table offers a quick reference guide for the main parts of speech.

Part of Speech	Function	Examples
noun	names a person, place, thing, or concept	*cloud, Helen, car, Elm Court, brush, valor*
verb	shows an action, occurrence, or state of being	*go, jump, feel, imagine, interrupt*
adjective	describes nouns and pronouns; can also identify or quantify; tells what kind, which one, how many, how much	*white, oblong, ancient, exhilarating* *that* (e.g., *that dog*) *several* (e.g., *several dogs*)
adverb	describes verbs, adjectives, other adverbs, or entire clauses; tells where, when, how and to what extent	*slowly, clumsily, never, very, here, soon*

For example, look how the suffixes in the following table change the word *antagonist* from a noun to an adjective to a verb (and don't forget to notice the prefix, *ant-*).

Word	Part of Speech	Definition
antagonist	noun	one who opposes or contends with another; an adversary, opponent
antagonistic	adjective	opposing, combating, adversarial
antagonize	verb	to oppose actively, contend; to provoke the hostility of

Likewise, the word *venerate* changes from a verb to an adjective to a noun, depending upon its suffix.

Word	Part of Speech	Definition
venerate	verb	to regard with deep respect or reverence; to honor with a sense of awe, revere
venerable	adjective	worthy of deep respect or reverence; deserving of honor and respect;
venerator	noun	one who shows deep respect or reverence

Again, just knowing suffixes won't enable you to determine the full meaning of an unfamiliar word, but it can help you determine the function of the word, zero in on its meaning, and eliminate incorrect answers on an exam. For example, if you know that the suffix *-ity* means state of being, you know that a word with this ending is probably a noun describing a state of being, such as *equality* (state of being equal). Similarly, if you know that *-ish* is a common suffix for adjectives, you can eliminate answer choices that do not match that part of speech.

Select the best answer to the question.

 *Squeamish* means
   a. to scream or squeal.
   b. recurring illness.
   c. extremely shy.
   d. easily disgusted.

Choices **a** and **b** are definitions for other parts of speech—a verb and a noun, respectively. Only choices **c** and **d** define adjectives, and only choice **d** is correct. *Squeamish* means easily sickened, disgusted, nauseated, or shocked.

HERE'S A HINT
MOST OF THE TIME, BUT NOT ALWAYS

While prefixes and suffixes are fundamental components of your vocabulary, it's important to remember that they are tools to use in conjunction with other vocabulary skills.

For example, most words that end in *-ish* are adjectives describing a characteristic. However, *vanquish* and *varnish* both end in *-ish,* but they are both verbs, not adjectives. Thus, as you come across vocabulary words with common prefixes and suffixes, use your knowledge of prefixes and suffixes, but look for other clues to meaning as well, including context (see Chapter 2) and word roots (see Chapter 4 and Appendix B) to be sure you are on the right track.

The following is a list of the suffixes you need to know for the practice questions at the end of the chapter. For each suffix, we have again provided two examples of words that use that suffix, and again, these examples are basic words that are part of your everyday vocabulary.

▶ Noun Suffixes

-ance, -ence: action, process, or state of
adolescence (the state of growing up from childhood to adulthood; the transitional period between youth and maturity), *dependence* (the state of being dependent)

-ian: one who is or does
comedian (one who creates comedy), *politician* (one who seeks or holds a political office)

-ion: act or process; state or condition
detection (the act of detecting), *election* (the act or power of electing)

-ism: act, practice, or process; state or doctrine of
feminism (belief in the social, political, and economic equality of the sexes), *materialism* (the belief that the acquisition of material possessions is the highest good)

-ist: one who performs, makes, produces, believes, etc.
dentist (one who is trained and licensed to practice dentistry), *pianist* (one who plays the piano)

-ity: quality, state, or degree
equality (the state or quality of being equal), *fidelity* (the quality of being faithful)

-sis: process or action
diagnosis (the process of identifying the nature or cause of a disease or injury), *paralysis* (loss of sensation or ability to move or function)

-ure: act, process, function
enclosure (an area or thing that is enclosed), *failure* (something that has failed to perform as expected or requested).

HERE'S A HINT
MEMORIZING PREFIXES AND SUFFIXES

You may try to save time by memorizing a difficult vocabulary word for each prefix or suffix. However, you can quickly and accurately learn the most common prefixes and suffixes by remembering examples of words you already know, such as *cooperate* and *dismiss*. Because the words are already so familiar to you, you don't have to worry about forgetting their meaning and you will be able to recall them easily even while under the pressure of an exam.

▶ Adjective Suffixes

-able, -ible: capable or worthy of; tending or liable to
dependable (worthy of being depended on, trustworthy), *incredible* (not credible; unable to be believed, improbable)

-al, -ial, -ical: having the quality of, relating to, or characterized by
practical (of or relating to practice or action; useful), *ethical* (of or relating to ethics or morals)

-an, -ian: related to, characteristic of
humanitarian (relating to, or characteristic of a humanitarian), *vegetarian* (relating to vegetarianism)

-ic: pertaining or relating to, having the quality of
dramatic (of or relating to drama, theatrical), *realistic* (of or relating to the representation of things as they really are)

-ile: having the qualities of
fragile (easily broken, damaged, or destroyed; frail), *servile* (pertaining to or befitting a slave; abjectly submissive, slavish)

-ish: having the character of
childish (characteristic of, pertaining to, or resembling a child), *foolish* (devoid of good sense or judgment; exhibiting folly, in the manner of a fool)

-ive: performing or tending towards (an action); having the nature of
cooperative (marked by a willingness to cooperate; done with or working with others for a common purpose), *defensive* (serving to defend or protect)

-ous, -ose: full of, having the quality of, relating to
glorious (having or deserving glory, famous), *nauseous* (causing nausea, sickening)

▶ Verb Suffixes

-ate: to make, cause to be or become
deteriorate (to make worse, impair; to make inferior in quality or character), *irritate* (to cause annoyance or disturbance in; to make impatient, angry, annoyed)

-ify, -fy: to make, form into
beautify (to make beautiful), *specify* (to state explicitly or in detail)

-ize: to cause to be or become, to bring about
colonize (to establish a colony), *democratize* (to make or become democratic)

TIPS AND STRATEGIES

A good knowledge of prefixes and suffixes is an invaluable asset when you are building your vocabulary and studying for the TOEFL iBT. Here are some specific tips and strategies to use as you develop this skill and prepare for your test.

- Take the time to memorize the most common prefixes and suffixes. By memorizing these essential word parts, you will be able to learn new words more quickly and better determine the meaning of unfamiliar words.
- Use words that you are very familiar with as examples when you study prefixes and suffixes. The more familiar the word is to you (e.g., *cooperate*), the easier it will be for you to remember the meaning of the prefix or suffix.
- Remember that you use prefixes and suffixes every day, all the time. Do not feel intimidated by the long lists in this chapter or in Appendix B. You already know much of this material.
- Remember that prefixes and suffixes alone do not create meaning; rather, they change or add to the meaning of the root word. Use as many

vocabulary skills as you can to determine meaning, including prefixes and suffixes, word roots (covered in the next chapter), and context.

- Allow for exceptions. Although most words ending in *-ist* are nouns defining a kind of person (one who does), not every *-ist* word is only a noun. *Elitist* is an example of an adjective with this ending. Check prefixes, word roots, and context if possible to confirm meaning.

- Use your knowledge of prefixes and suffixes to eliminate incorrect answers. The more you narrow down your choices, the better your chances of choosing the correct answer.

- Once you have narrowed down your answer choices, determine the part of speech of each remaining choice. Does it match the part of speech of the definition according to the suffix?

- If you know the prefix or suffix but still aren't sure of a word's meaning, try to recall another word with a similar root. Plug in that meaning with the prefix or suffix and see if it makes sense.

PRACTICE QUESTIONS

Directions: Choose the best answer to each question using your knowledge of prefixes and suffixes. Circle your choices or write your answers on a separate piece of paper. Then compare your selections to the correct answers at the end of the chapter.

1. *Antecedent* means
   a. fighting against.
   b. looking after.
   c. coming before.
   d. under the authority of.

2. *Multifaceted* means
   a. two-faced.
   b. many sided.
   c. uniform.
   d. cut into parts.

3. *Circumspect* means
   a. relating to the circus.
   b. to examine thoroughly.
   c. put forth in writing.
   d. looking around carefully.

4. *Consensus* means
   a. general agreement by a group.
   b. an individual opinion.
   c. a counting of individuals.
   d. to issue a warning.

5. *Supercilious* means
   a. less than the norm, disappointing.
   b. exactly as expected.
   c. speaking in a measured, exact tone.
   d. haughty, with an air of superiority.

6. To *presage* means
   a. to warn in advance.
   b. to send a message.
   c. to pressure.
   d. to age gracefully.

7. *Dubious* means
   a. one who doubts, a nonbeliever.
   b. to doubt or question.
   c. doubtful, questionable.
   d. to be uncertain.

8. *Agrarian* means
   a. incapable of making a decision.
   b. to cultivate.
   c. to be out of date.
   d. relating to land or land ownership.

9. *Parity* means
   a. to make equal in status, amount, or degree.
   b. the state of being equal in status, amount, or degree.
   c. one who is equal in status, amount, or degree.
   d. the act of making someone or something equal in status, amount, or degree.

10. *Galvanize* means
    a. to be active or aware.
    b. the state of becoming active or aware.
    c. one who becomes active or aware.
    d. to cause to become active or aware.

11. *Nonchalant* means
    a. challenging.
    b. done with the intent of harming another.
    c. not showing anxiety or excitement; indifferent.
    d. reversing a previous opinion or decision.

ANSWERS

How did you do on remembering prefixes and suffixes? Check your answers here, and then analyze the results to figure out your plan of attack for mastering these topics.

1. **c.** The prefix *ante-* means before. *Antecedent* means that which precedes; the thing, circumstance, or event that came before.
2. **b.** The prefix *multi-* means many. *Multifaceted* means having many facets or aspects; complex.
3. **d.** The prefix *circum-* means around, on all sides. *Circumspect* means cautious, wary, watchful.
4. **a.** The prefix *con-* means with, together. *Consensus* means general agreement or accord; an opinion or position reached by a group.
5. **d.** The prefix *super-* means above, over, or exceeding. *Supercilious* means with an air of superiority (as if one is above or better than another); haughty, scornful, disdainful.
6. **a.** The prefix *pre-* means before. To *presage* means to indicate or warn of in advance; to predict, foretell.
7. **c.** The adjective suffix *-ous* means having the quality of, relating to. *Dubious* means doubtful, questionable; fraught with uncertainty, wavering.
8. **d.** The adjective suffix *-ian* means related to. *Agrarian* means relating to or concerning land and its ownership or cultivation.
9. **b.** The noun suffix *-ity* means state of being. *Parity* means having equality in status, amount, value or degree; equivalence.
10. **d.** The verb suffix *-ize* means to cause, to bring about. To *galvanize* means to stimulate or rouse into awareness or action.
11. **c.** The prefix *non-* means not. *Nonchalant* means indifferent or cool, not showing anxiety or excitement.

Word Roots

Prefixes and suffixes attach to word roots—the base parts of words that typically convey the bulk of their meaning. The more word roots you know, the more you will be able to determine the meaning of unfamiliar words and the better you will understand words you already know. This chapter examines some common Latin and Greek word roots.

Just as many Americans have their roots in other countries, so, too, do many of the words in the English language. In fact, most English words have been borrowed from other languages throughout the centuries, and English is composed largely of words built upon root words from other cultures. The two most important categories of roots to learn are Latin and Greek roots because so many English words are built upon Latin and Greek word bases. For example, *manual* and *manufacture* share the Latin root *man*, meaning hand; *anonymous* and *synonym* share the Greek root *nom/nym*, meaning name.

Needless to say, the more roots you know, the stronger your vocabulary will be. As you break down unfamiliar words into their parts, you will be more likely to recognize the roots and therefore more accurately determine meaning. You will also have a better understanding of the words you already know.

Just as you can better understand a person by learning about that person's past, you can also better understand words and more effectively build your vocabulary by learning about the history of words. The study of word origins and development is called **etymology**. When you break down a word and identify a root word from another language, you are tracing the etymology or history of that word.

DEFINITION

etymology: the history of a word, the study of its origin and development

Many words have a rich history, and a detailed etymological study will show you not only where a word comes from but also how its meaning has changed over time. For now, however, the focus of this chapter remains on learning some of the most common roots so that you can better determine meaning and succeed on the TOEFL iBT.

HERE'S A HINT
MNEMONICS

Don't let the spelling of this word scare you! Mnemonics is a simple concept. Meaning "memory aid," mnemonics can be handy for helping you remember a word's root word, meaning, or spelling. The idea behind mnemonics is that people remember best when more than one function of the brain is used to process information.

Simple mnemonics can be created from rhymes, tunes, or acronyms (words that are made up of the first letters of a group of words or phrases. For example, the acronym *Roy G. Biv* is a mnemonic used when learning the colors of the spectrum (red, orange, yellow, green, blue, indigo, violet). Mental pictures and stories are also useful mnemonics.

Use mnemonic devices to remember the meaning of word roots. For example, you can use the following sentences to remember these roots:

Root	Meaning	Sentence
nomen	name	My name is *Nom*.
herb	plants	My mother plants *herbs* in her garden.
graph	write	He will write the information on a *graph*.
pan	all	All the eggs are in the *pan*.
phil	love	*Phil* loves to help others.

Here's a trick to remember the difference between *hetero* (different) and *homo* (same): *homo* has the same number of letters as *same*.

Here are some tips on creating mnemonics that will be easy to remember and, therefore, useful:

- Use rhymes, rhythmic patterns, or tunes.
- Try humorous or odd sayings that will stick in your mind.
- Exaggerate features or images to make them vivid.
- Make your mnemonics personally meaningful.

On occasion, Latin and Greek roots are themselves words. The Latin roots *err* and *pug*, for example, mean to make a mistake and a boxer, respectively. But most of the time, roots are the base to which prefixes and suffixes (and sometimes other roots) are attached to create a rich variety of meaning. Look at the etymology of the word *homogeneous:*

homo: Greek root meaning *same*
gen: Latin root meaning *birth, kind*
ous: suffix meaning *having the quality of, related to*

Thus, *homogeneous* (also spelled *homogenous*) means of the *same* or similar nature or *kind;* having a uniform structure or composition throughout.

Now, take the Latin root *ced/ceed/cess,* meaning to go, yield, stop. Notice how many different words can be created by adding different prefixes and suffixes to this root and how the different prefixes and suffixes change meaning.

ante**ced**ent: that which precedes or comes before
cessation: a stopping, a bringing to an end
con**cede**: to acknowledge or admit as true, proper, etc. (often with reluctance); to yield, surrender
con**cess**ion: the act of conceding or yielding; a thing yielded, an acknowledgement or admission
ex**ceed**: to extend beyond or outside of; surpass
pre**cede**: to come or go before in time, place, rank, or importance
prede**cess**or: one who precedes or comes before another in time (as in holding an office or position)
pro**ceed**: to go forward or onward, especially after an interruption; move on, advance
pro**ced**ure: the act or manner of proceeding; a course of action or conduct; process

Now, try determining what the word *recede* means:

    a. to go forward blindly
    b. to stop or abandon before completion
    c. to move or go back, retreat
    d. to go together with others

Remember your prefixes from Chapter 3. *Re-* means back, again; *ced* means to go, yield, stop. *Recede* means **c**, to move back, withdraw, retreat. Now add the noun suffix *-sion*, meaning the act or state of, and you get:

➡   *recession:* the act of withdrawing or going back

With your knowledge of prefixes and suffixes, you can also answer the following question.

➡   *Incessant* means
    a. yielding readily under pressure.
    b. not stopping, continuing without interruption.
    c. to move or go below the surface, subliminal.
    d. going between, through, or among; not direct.

The correct answer is **b**. The prefix *in-* means not; *cess* means to go, stop, or yield; and the suffix *-ant* means being in a state or condition of; performing or causing an action. Thus, *incessant* means continuing without interruption; ceaseless, continuous.

Here are several words formed from another Latin root, *plac*, meaning to please. Again, notice the rich variety of meaning created by adding different prefixes and suffixes to the root word.

placate: to appease, pacify; to allay the anger of, especially by making concessions
im**plac**able: incapable of being placated or appeased; inexorable
placid: calm and peaceful; free from disturbance or tumult
com**plac**ent: contented to a fault; self-satisfied, unconcerned
placebo: an inactive, harmless substance of no medicinal value given to patients to reassure them or to members of a control group in experiments testing the efficacy of a drug

HERE'S A HINT
MAKE THE MOST OF YOUR LEARNING STYLE

For many people, especially visual learners, the best way to memorize words is to create a picture in the mind associated with that word. For example, to remember the root *pug*, you might picture a pug dog in a boxing ring, or a boxer with a pug nose. Similarly, you might picture a stop sign with the root *ced* written on it instead of *stop*, or a yield sign with *cess* instead of *yield*. You could also picture a traffic light for the root *ced/ceed/cess*, because the colors of the traffic light correspond with the three meanings of this root: go, stop, yield. If you are a visual learner, again, use pictures to help you remember words. To remember that *eu* means good or well, you can picture the letters EU on a well.

If you are an auditory learner, you can come up with rhymes or short sentences to help you remember root meanings. For example, you could try one of these sentences for the root *am,* meaning love:

I *am* love.
I love *Am*y.
I love h*am*.

Many different words can be built from a single root. For example, look at the number of words and the rich variety of meaning that comes from the Greek root *chron*, meaning time.

chronic: continuing for a long time; on-going, habitual; long-lasting or recurrent
chronology: the arrangement of events in time; the sequence in which events occurred
chronicle: a detailed record or narrative description of past events; to record in chronological order, make a historical record
chronological: relating to chronology; arranged in order of time of occurrence
chronometer: an exceptionally accurate clock; a precise instrument for measuring time
syn**chron**ize: to cause to occur at the same time or agree in time; to occur at the same time, be simultaneous

By changing the suffix of *synchronize*, we can create even more words. For example, we can turn it into the noun *synchronicity*, which is the state or fact of being *synchronous*, an adjective that means occurring or existing at the same time.

What follows is a list of some of the most common Latin and Greek word roots. Review the list carefully, taking note of the examples, which once again are mostly everyday words. A more comprehensive list of the most common Latin and Greek word roots is located in Appendix B. After you have completed this lesson, make sure you review the list carefully and study any roots that are unfamiliar to you.

COMMON LATIN WORD ROOTS

ac, acr: sharp, bitter
acid (something that is sharp, sour, or ill natured), *acute* (extremely sharp or severe; keenly perceptive)

am: love
amorous (inclined to love; romantic, affectionate), *enamored* (inflamed or inspired by love; captivated)

bel: war
antebellum (before the war, especially the American Civil War), *rebel* (to resist or defy authority)

cast, chast: cut
caste (a social class separated from others by hereditary rank, profession, etc.), *chastise* (to punish severely, as with a beating; to rebuke)

ced, ceed, cess: to go, yield, stop
antecedent (that which precedes), *exceed* (to extend beyond or outside of; surpass)

culp: blame
culprit (person accused or guilty of a crime), *mea culpa* (Latin, "my fault")

dic, dict, dit: to say, tell, use words
dictate (to say or read aloud; to issue orders or commands), *predict* (to foretell, make known in advance)

equ: equal, even
equate (to make or consider two things as equal), *equidistant* (equally distant)

err: to wander
err (to make a mistake), *error* (a mistake; an incorrect or wrong action)

ferv: to boil, bubble, burn
fervid (very hot, burning; ardent, vehement), *effervescent* (bubbling up, as a carbonated liquid; high spirited, animated)

loc, log, loqu: word, speech
dialogue (a conversation between two or more people), *neologism* (a new word or phrase)

luc, lum, lus: light
illuminate (to brighten with light; enlighten), *translucent* (almost transparent; allowing light to pass through diffusely)

lug, lut, luv: to wash
dilute (to make thinner or weaker by adding a liquid such as water; to lessen the force or purity of), *pollute* (to make impure or unclean; to make unfit or harmful to living things)

mag, maj, max: big
magnify (to increase in size, volume or significance; to amplify), *maximum* (the greatest possible quantity or degree)

man: hand
manual (operated by hand), *manufacture* (to make by hand or machinery)

min: to project, hang over
prominent (standing out, conspicuous; projecting or jutting beyond the line or surface), *eminent* (towering above or more prominent that others; lofty, distinguished)

nas, nat, nai: to be born
native (a person born in a particular country), *innate* (possessed at birth; inborn, inherent)

nec, nic, noc, nox: harm, death
innocent (uncorrupted by evil; free from guilt; not dangerous or harmful), *obnoxious* (offensive, hateful)

omni: all
omnipresent (everywhere at once), *omnipotent* (all powerful)

plac: to please
placid (calm and peaceful), *placate* (to appease or pacify)

pon, pos, pound: to put, place
deposit (to put or set down; place), *transpose* (to reverse or transfer the order or
place of; interchange)

pug: to fight
pug (a boxer), *repugnant* (highly offensive or distasteful; hostile, disposed to
fight)

qui: quiet
quiet (making little or no noise; calm, still), *tranquil* (free from disturbance,
anxiety, or tension)

rog: to ask
interrogate (to examine by asking a series of questions), *prerogative* (an exclusive privilege or right belonging to a person or group)

sci: to know
conscious (knowing and perceiving, aware), *science* (knowledge, especially that
gained through systematic study)

tac, tic: to be silent
tacit (not spoken; implied), *taciturn* (habitually untalkative, reserved)

ver: truth
verdict (the findings of a jury in a trial; decision or judgment), *verify* (to confirm the truth of)

vi: life
vivid (evoking lifelike images in the mind; true to life; bright, brilliant, distinct), *vigorous* (energetic, forceful, active, strong)

voc, vok: to call
vocal (of or pertaining to the voice; tending to express oneself often and freely,
outspoken), *revoke* (to cancel, call back, reverse, withdraw)

HERE'S A HINT
SYNONYMS AND ANTONYMS

Some TOEFL test questions ask you to find the synonym or antonym of a word. If you are lucky, the word will be surrounded by a sentence that helps you guess what the word means (this is vocabulary in context), but the test question could list just a synonym or antonym and four answer choices. In this case, you have to figure out what the word means without any help from context clues. Questions that ask for synonyms and antonyms can be difficult because they require you to have a relatively large vocabulary. Not only do you need to know the word in question, but you may be faced with four choices that are unfamiliar to you, too.

Usually the best strategy is to look at the structure of the word. See if a part of the word—the root—looks familiar. Often you will be able to determine the meaning of a word within the root. For instance, the root of *credible* is *cred,* which means to trust or believe. Knowing this, you will be able to understand the meaning of *incredible, sacred,* and *credit.* Looking for related words that have the same root as the word in question can help you choose the correct answer—even if it is by process of elimination.

Another way to dissect meaning is to look for prefixes and suffixes. Prefixes come before the word root, and suffixes are found at the end of a word. Either of these elements can carry meaning or change the use of a word in a sentence. For instance, the prefix can change the meaning of a root word to its opposite: *necessary, unnecessary.*

A suffix like *-less* can change the meaning of a noun: *pain* to *painless.* To identify most word parts—word root, prefix, or suffix—the best strategy is to think of words you already know that carry the same root, suffix, or prefix. Let what you know about those words help you find the meaning of words that are less familiar.

Antonym questions can be problematic because you can easily forget that you are looking for *opposites* and mistakenly choose the synonym. Very often, synonyms will be included as answer choices for antonym questions. The secret is to keep your mind on the fact that you are looking for the opposite of the word given in the question. If you are completing practice exercises like those in this book, circle the word *antonym* or *opposite* in the directions to help you remember.

Otherwise, the same tactics that work for synonym questions work for antonyms as well. Try to determine the meaning of part of the word, or try to remember a context where you have seen the word before.

COMMON GREEK WORD ROOTS

anthro, andro: man, human

android (a very humanlike machine or robot, especially one made of biological materials), *anthropology* (the social science that studies the origins and social relationships of human beings)

arch, archi, archy: chief, principal, ruler

architect (one who plans or devises; one who creates plans for buildings), *monarchy* (a state ruled by a monarch—a sole and absolute ruler, such as a king)

auto: self

automatic (operating without external influence or control; having inherent power of action or motion), *autopsy* (examination of a dead body to determine cause of death; seeing with one's own eyes)

card, cord, cour: heart

cardiac (of or relating to the heart), *encourage* (to inspire with hope, courage, or confidence; to give support, hearten)

chron: time

chronic (continuing for a long time; ongoing, habitual; long-lasting or recurrent), *chronology* (the arrangement of events in time; the sequence in which events occurred)

cli, clin: to lean toward, bend

incline (to lean, slant, slope, or cause to do so; to have a tendency or disposition toward something), *recline* (to lie back or down)

cryp: hidden

crypt (an underground vault or chamber, especially one used as a burial place), *cryptography* (secret writing; the process or skill of communicating in or deciphering coded messages)

dem: people

democracy (government by the people through elected representatives), *epidemic* (a widespread outbreak of a disease affecting many people at the same time)

di, dia: apart, through

diameter (a straight line passing through the center of a circle; thickness, width), *digress* (to turn aside, deviate, or swerve; to stray from the main subject in writing or speaking)

dog, dox: opinion

dogged (stubbornly unyielding, obstinate), *dogma* (a system of principles or beliefs, a prescribed doctrine)

dys: faulty, abnormal

dysfunctional (impaired or abnormal in function), *dyslexia* (an impaired ability to read)

eu: good, well

eulogy (a verbal or written tribute, especially one praising someone who has died), *euthanasia* (the act of painlessly ending the life of someone suffering from a terminal illness)

(h)etero: different, other

heterosexual (a person sexually attracted to members of the opposite sex), *heterodox* (disagreeing with or departing from accepted beliefs)

(h)omo: same

homogeneous (of the same or similar nature or kind; having a uniform structure or composition throughout), *homophone* (a word that sounds the same as another but has a different meaning)

hyper: over, excessive

hyperactive (highly or excessively active), *hyperventilate* (to breathe excessively and abnormally fast)

morph: shape

metamorphosis (a transformation, a marked change of form, character, or function), *polymorphous* (having or assuming a variety of forms)

nom, nym: name

nominate (to name as a candidate), *synonym* (a word having the same or nearly the same meaning as another)

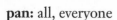

pan: all, everyone

panorama (a complete view in every direction), *pantheon* (a temple dedicated to all the gods; all the gods of a people or region)

pas, pat, path: feeling, suffering, disease

compassion (deep awareness of and sympathy for another's suffering), *sympathy* (sharing another person's feelings; feeling pity or tenderness toward another's pain or suffering; harmony, agreement between two people)

ped: education, child

encyclopedia (a comprehensive reference work on a wide range of subjects), *pediatrician* (a physician specializing in the care of infants and children)

peri: around

perimeter (the outer limits or boundary of an area), *periscope* (an optical instrument that provides a view of an otherwise obstructed field)

phil: love

bibliophile (a lover of books), *philosophy* (love and pursuit of wisdom; a systematic investigation of questions about knowledge, existence, and ethics)

phone: sound

phonics (a method of teaching reading by training beginners to associate letters with their sound values), *symphony* (a long and complex sonata for an orchestra; a large orchestra)

theo: god, religion

atheist (one who denies the existence of a god or supreme being), *theology* (the study of god(s) and religion)

When working on your vocabulary, remember to focus first on roots, prefixes, and suffixes. You will be surprised to see how quickly learning these will increase the size of your vocabulary.

 HERE'S A HINT
TRY DIFFERENT APPROACHES

Not everyone "sees" words in the same way. You might, for example, respond to a visual clue in a word, or you might instead hear a familiar sound in that word. Another person reading that same word might recognize a structural clue in the word; for instance, she might grasp its meaning by associating the word's prefix with that same prefix on another word she knows. The bottom line is that because you can't be sure which strategy will work for you or when, try them all!

THE POWER OF ASSOCIATION

Need more help memorizing word roots? Use the power of association. A *rebel*, for example, fights in a war; the meaning of the root *bel* is war. The *acute* pain you felt in your ankle when you sprained it was very sharp; the root *ac* means sharp, bitter.

Similarly, as you are learning roots and trying to determine the meaning of unfamiliar words, especially on an exam like the TOEFL iBT, think of other words that sound like they might share a root word. For example, if you don't know the meaning of *amiable* but you do know what *enamored* means, you can at least determine that *amiable* is probably a positive thing and that it probably has something to do with love or friendship.

Now you have the tools to really break down words and work out their meanings. By memorizing common prefixes, suffixes, and word roots, you will be able to accurately guess the meaning of many unfamiliar words, and this will both dramatically expand your vocabulary and significantly improve your score on the TOEFL iBT.

HERE'S A HINT
USE WORD PARTS

Remember to use word parts to help you determine and remember meaning. For example, *fervent* has the root *ferv,* which means to boil, bubble, burn. The prefix *im-* in *impervious* means not, and this tells you that *impervious* means *not pervious*.

TIPS AND STRATEGIES

Many words in the English language come from Latin or Greek word roots. Here again are some specific strategies for using your knowledge of word roots to build your vocabulary and improve your vocabulary skills. When you are faced with an unfamiliar word in your reading or on an exam, your best strategy is to break it down into its parts and look for a familiar word root. Here are some specific strategies for sharpening this skill and using it in a test situation.

- Take the time to memorize as many Latin and Greek roots as you can. By memorizing these word bases, you will be able to learn new words more quickly and better determine the meaning of unfamiliar words.

- Use words that you are very familiar with as examples when you study word roots. The more familiar the word is to you (e.g., *predict*, *equate*), the easier it will be for you to remember the meaning of the root word. Or use words that create a vivid picture in your imagination.

- Remember that you use common word roots every day, often without realizing it. Do not feel intimidated by the long lists in this chapter or in Appendix B. You already know much of this material.

- Remember that word roots work with prefixes and suffixes—and sometimes other root words—to create meaning. Look at all parts of the word and the context, if possible, to determine meaning.

- Remember the power of elimination on an exam. Use your knowledge of word roots to eliminate incorrect answers. The more you narrow down your choices, the better your chances of choosing the correct answer.

- Use the power of association. If you don't know or can't remember the root word, try to recall the meaning of another word with a similar root.

PRACTICE QUESTIONS

For each question, use the word root to determine the meaning of the italicized word. Circle your choices or write your answers on a separate piece of paper. Then compare your selections to the correct answers at the end or the chapter.

1. An *amiable* person is
   a. talkative, loud.
   b. truthful, honest.
   c. highly educated.
   d. friendly, good natured.

2. A *lucid* argument
   a. is very clear and intelligible.
   b. is loosely held together, tenuous.
   c. frequently digresses.
   d. errs repeatedly in its logic.

3. A *complacent* person
    a. frequently makes mistakes, but does not accept responsibility.
    b. likes to pick fights.
    c. is contented to a fault, self-satisfied.
    d. is known to tell lies, embellish the truth.

4. To *exacerbate* a problem means
    a. to solve it.
    b. to analyze it.
    c. to lessen it.
    d. to worsen it.

5. To measure the *veracity* of something is to measure its
    a. value or worth.
    b. truthfulness.
    c. weight.
    d. circumference.

6. Something that is *eloquent* is
    a. dull, trite, hackneyed.
    b. expressed in a powerful and effective manner.
    c. very old, antiquated.
    d. not fit for consumption, inedible.

7. To *indict* someone is to
    a. pick a fight with that person.
    b. stop or block that person from doing something.
    c. harm that person.
    d. charge that person with a crime.

8. A *quiescent* place is
    a. very isolated.
    b. tumultuous, chaotic.
    c. harmful, dangerous.
    d. still, at rest.

9. A *noxious* odor is
  a. harmful.
  b. unscented.
  c. tantalizing.
  d. refreshing.

10. A person with *equanimity*
  a. has a violent temper.
  b. is very stubborn.
  c. enjoys the company of others.
  d. is even-tempered and composed.

ANSWERS

How did you do on identifying word roots? Check your answers here, and then analyze the results to figure out your plan of attack for mastering this topic.

1. **d.** The root *am* means love. *Amiable* means friendly and agreeable; good natured, likeable, pleasing.
2. **a.** The root *luc/lum/lus* means light. *Lucid* means very clear, easy to understand, intelligible.
3. **c.** The root *plac* means to please. *Complacent* means contented to a fault; self-satisfied (pleased with oneself).
4. **d.** The root *ac* means sharp, bitter. To *exacerbate* means to make worse; to increase the severity, violence, or bitterness of.
5. **b.** The root *ver* means truth. *Veracity* means truth, truthfulness.
6. **b.** The root *loc/log/loqu* means word, speech. *Eloquent* means expressed in a powerful, fluent, and persuasive manner.
7. **d.** The root *dic/dict/dit* means to say, tell, use words. To *indict* means to formally accuse of or charge with a crime.
8. **d.** The root *qui* means quiet. *Quiescent* means inactive, quiet, at rest.
9. **a.** The root *nec/nic/noc/nox* means harm, death. *Noxious* means unpleasant and harmful, unwholesome.
10. **d.** The root *equ* means equal, even. *Equanimity* means calmness of temperament, even-temperedness; patience and composure, especially under stress.

5

Commonly Confused Words—Homonyms

Do you know when *nail* means something used with a hammer and when it means a part of your finger? When to use *ensure* instead of *assure*? *Incredulous* instead of *incredible*? Using the right word can make the difference between confusion and clarity—and have a huge impact on your TOEFL iBT score. This chapter reviews commonly confused words that you might encounter on your TOEFL iBT.

One thing to watch for are words that sound the same and may look alike but mean different things. They are called **homonyms**. For example, the word *season* has several meanings:

➡ a part of the year (n): spring, summer, fall, or winter
➡ to flavor food (v): *I will season the sauce with some curry.*
➡ to make experienced (v): *Several months touring with a jazz band will season a young trumpet player because every night, he will learn something new about his craft.*

The term *homonym* comes from Greek roots meaning:

homo (same)
nym (name)

A specific type of homonyms are called **homographs**—words that look alike but that sound different and mean different things. Notice that the different sound in these words can come from the accent, or stress, on one part of the word. For example, *conduct* has two distinct meanings and pronunciations:

➡ kun-DUKT (v) means to lead or direct. *I will conduct the orchestra for the last song.*

➡ KON-dukt (n) means behavior. *His conduct in school was terrible.*

Another type of homonyms are pronounced the same way, but have different spellings and meanings. The term for these words, **homophone**, is exactly what its two Greek roots suggest:

homo (same)
phone (sound)

It is a word that sounds the same as another but has a different meaning. *Night* and *knight*, for example, are homophones, as are *slay* and *sleigh*, *great* and *grate*, and *bear* and *bare*. There are dozens of homophones, many of which you may already know, while others that you may still find confusing. If so, this chapter will help you get them straight.

 DEFINITION

homonyms: a group of words that share the same spelling or pronunciation (or both) but have different meanings

Standardized tests, like TOEFL iBT, will often test you on the correct homonym for a given context—whether you should use *whether* or *weather* in a sentence, for example, or *piece* or *peace*. It is very important to know your homonyms and use them correctly. Otherwise, you may confuse your readers with sentences that are at best incorrect and at worst unintelligible. So take some time to review the following list of frequently confused words carefully.

FREQUENTLY CONFUSED WORDS

The following table lists some of the most frequently confused word pairs along with a brief definition of each word.

CONFUSING WORDS	QUICK DEFINITION
accept	to recognize
except	excluding
access (verb)	to gain entry to
access (noun)	means of approaching
excess	extra
adapt	to adjust
adopt	to take as one's own
affect	to influence
effect (noun)	result
effect (verb)	to bring about
all ready	totally prepared
already	by this time
all ways	every method
always	forever
among	in the middle of several
between	in an interval separating (two)
assure	to make certain (assure someone)
ensure	to make certain (to check for yourself)
insure	to make certain (financial value)
beside	next to
besides	in addition to
bibliography	list of writings
biography	a life story

CONFUSING WORDS	QUICK DEFINITION
breath (noun)	respiration
breathe (verb)	to inhale and exhale
breadth	width
capital (noun)	money
capital (adjective)	most important
capitol	government building
complement (noun, verb)	match
compliment (noun, verb)	praise
disinterested	no strong opinion either way
uninterested	unengaged; having no interest in
envelop	to surround
envelope	paper wrapping for a letter
farther	beyond
further	additional
immigrate	to enter a new country
emigrate	to leave a country
imply	to hint, suggest
infer	to assume, deduce
its	belonging to it
it's	it is
loose	not tight
lose	unable to find
may be	something may possibly be
maybe	perhaps
overdo	to do too much
overdue	late

CONFUSING WORDS	QUICK DEFINITION
personal	individual
personnel	employees
precede	to go before
proceed	to continue
proceeds	profits
principal (adjective)	main
principal (noun)	person in charge; sum of interest-earning money
principle	standard
stationary	still, not moving
stationery	writing material
than	in contrast to
then	next in time
their	belonging to them
there	in a place
they're	they are
weather	climate
whether	if
who	substitute for *he, she,* or *they*
whom	substitute for *him, her,* or *them*
whose	belonging to whom
who's	who is
your	belonging to you
you're	you are

Another important reason to review homonyms like *team/teem* and *waive/wave* is to avoid a "trap" sometimes set by the test developers. That is, you might encounter questions that use the definition of a familiar homonym as a distracter. Here's an example:

> To *waive* means
> **a.** to signal with an up and down or back and forth movement.
> **b.** to return to the original starting point.
> **c.** to relinquish a right or claim.
> **d.** to swell up or rise to the surface.

The correct answer is **c**. *Waive* means to give up (a right or claim) voluntarily, relinquish; to refrain from enforcing or insisting upon (a rule, penalty, standard procedure, etc.). If you don't know the meaning of *waive*, however, you might be tempted to choose **a**, which is the definition of its homophone *wave*, or **d**, which is related to the definition of a wave. These answer choices are tempting because they sound familiar. You need to be able to recognize the familiar homophone and recall its definition.

Not all commonly confused words are homonyms. Take *disinterested* and *uninterested* as an example. They don't sound the same because they have very distinct prefixes. But the prefixes are attached to the same root, and the prefixes seem to have essentially the same meaning: *dis-* means away from, apart, reversal, not; *un-* means not, against. Thus many people assume that both words mean the same thing: *not* interested. However, only *uninterested* has this meaning. *Disinterested* means impartial or unbiased, free of selfish motives or interests—a different word entirely.

Some commonly confused words are particularly puzzling because the words not only sound similar, but they also have similar meanings. Take the homophones *cue* and *queue*, for example. Both mean a line of waiting people or vehicles, although *queue* is used far more often than *cue* for this meaning. However, *cue* also means a signal, such as a word or action, given to prompt or remind someone of something—and this is its most common usage. And *queue* can also mean an ordered list of tasks to be performed or sequence of programs awaiting processing on a computer.

HERE'S A HINT
TRICKY VERBS

These verbs confuse even native speakers of English. To keep them straight, think about which verb in a pair needs an object (a noun or pronoun that's acted on by a verb). Practice using these verbs in context and you will become more comfortable with them.

Lie	Lay
Lie means to rest, to recline.	*Lay* means to place, to set down.
(subject)	(needs an object)
past tense: *lay, had lain*	*I always lay my purse on the table.*
Don't just lie there, do something!	

Sit	Set
Sit means to rest.	*Set* means to put or place.
(subject)	(needs an object)
She always sits in the third row.	*He set the newspaper on the desk.*

Rise	Raise
Rise means to go up.	*Raise* means to move something up.
(subject)	(needs an object)
After it is filled with helium, the balloon rises.	*The state is raising taxes this year.*

You already know many homophones and commonly confused words inside and out. The ones you don't know, you simply need to memorize. The question is, how do you remember these differences in meaning, especially when the words seem so much alike? The key is to capitalize on the differences in the words. And when it comes to frequently confused words, mnemonic devices come in especially handy. Take the commonly confused pair *ingenious* and *ingenuous*, for example:

➡ **ingenious**: marked by inventive skill or creativity; showing inventiveness and skill, remarkably clever
➡ **ingenuous**: 1. not cunning or deceitful, unable to mask feelings; artless, frank, sincere. 2. lacking sophistication or worldliness

The only difference in the spelling of these words is the *i/u*. You can use this difference to remember key words in the definition of each word.

➡ **ingenious**: inventive
➡ **ingenuous**: unable to mask feelings

Similarly, the difference between *disinterested* and *uninterested* is the prefix. Use this to help you remember the meaning: a *dis*interested person is *dis*tanced from the situation and is therefore impartial.

Here is a list of more commonly confused word sets that include important vocabulary words for your TOEFL iBT test preparation.

allude (ă·'lood) *v.* to make an indirect reference to
elude (i·'lood) *v.* 1. to escape from or evade, especially by cleverness, daring, or skill. 2. to be incomprehensible to, escape the understanding of

appraise (ă·'prayz) *v.* 1. to evaluate. 2. to establish value or estimate the worth of
apprise (ă·'prīz) *v.* to give notice or information to; to make aware of, inform

ascent (ă·'sent) *n.* 1. an upward slope. 2. a movement upward, advancement
assent (ă·'sent) *n.* agreement; concurrence; consent

censor ('sen·sŏr) *v.* to forbid the publication, distribution, or other public dissemination of something because it is considered obscene or otherwise politically or morally unacceptable. *n.* an official who reviews books, films, etc. to remove what is considered morally, politically, or otherwise objectionable
censure ('sen·shŭr) *n.* expression of strong criticism or disapproval; a rebuke or condemnation. *v.* to criticize strongly, rebuke, condemn
sensor ('sen·sŏr) *n.* a device that receives and responds to a stimulus such as light, smoke, etc.

cue (kyoo) *n.* 1. a signal, such as a word or action, given to prompt or remind someone of something; a hint or suggestion. 2. a line of waiting people or vehicles; a queue
queue (kyoo) *n.* 1. a line of waiting people or vehicles. 2. (in information processing) an ordered list of tasks to be performed or sequence of programs awaiting processing

decent ('dee·sĕnt) *adj.* 1. conforming to what is socially or morally suitable or correct. 2. meeting acceptable standards; sufficient, adequate

descent (di·'sent) *n.* 1. the act of descending or moving downward; a downward slope or movement. 2. hereditary derivation; lineage

dissent (di·'sent) *v.* 1. to differ in opinion, disagree. 2. to withhold approval or assent. *n.* 1. a difference of opinion. 2. nonconformity

deprecate ('dep·rĕ·kayt) *v.* to express disapproval of; to belittle, depreciate

depreciate (di·'pree·shi·ayt) *v.* 1. to diminish in price or value; to lessen the worth of. 2. to think or speak of as being of little worth; to belittle

disburse (dis·'burs) *v.* to pay out

disperse (dis·'spurs) *v.* 1. to separate and scatter in different directions; to cause to do so. 2. to distribute widely, disseminate

elicit (i·'lis·it) *v.* 1. to call forth or draw out; to provoke. 2. to deduce or derive by reasoning

illicit (i·'lis·it) *adj.* illegal, forbidden by law; contrary to accepted morality or convention

eminent ('em·ĭ·nĕnt) *adj.* towering above or more prominent than others, lofty; standing above others in quality, character, reputation, etc.; distinguished

imminent ('im·ĭ·nĕnt) *adj.* about to occur; impending

emanate ('em·ă·nayt) *v.* to come or issue forth, as from a source

extant ('ek·stănt) *adj.* still in existence; not extinct, destroyed or lost

extent (ik·'stent) *n.* the range, distance, or degree to which something reaches or extends. 2. a wide and open space or area

fain (fayn) *adv.* with joy; gladly

feign (fayn) *v.* to pretend, to give the false appearance of

faux (foh) *adj.* artificial, fake; not genuine or real

foe (foh) *n.* an enemy, adversary, or opponent

hoard (hohrd) *n.* a hidden store or stock, cache. *v.* to collect and lay up; to amass and store in secret

horde (hohrd) *n.* a large group or crowd; a vast multitude

incredible (in·ˈkred·ĭ·bĕl) *adj.* 1. implausible, beyond belief. 2. astonishing
incredulous (in·ˈkrej·ŭ·lŭs) *adj.* skeptical, unwilling to believe

ingenious (in·ˈjeen·yŭs) *adj.* marked by inventive skill or creativity; showing inventiveness and skill, remarkably clever
ingenuous (in·ˈjen·yoo·ŭs) *adj.* 1. not cunning or deceitful, unable to mask feelings; artless, frank, sincere. 2. lacking sophistication or worldliness

meddle (ˈmed·ĕl) *v.* to intrude in other people's affairs; interfere
mettle (ˈmet·ĕl) *n.* courage, fortitude, spirit

peak (peek) *v.* to reach its highest point or maximum development, activity, or intensity. *n.* 1. the sharp end of something tapering to a point. 2. the pointed top of a mountain, summit. 3. the highest possible point of development, activity, or intensity
peek (peek) *v.* to glance quickly or peer at furtively. *n.* a brief or furtive look.
pique (peek) *v.* 1. to cause annoyance or irritation; to vex or create resentment. 2. to provoke or arouse

persecute (ˈpur·sĕ·kyoot) *v.* to oppress, harass, or mistreat, especially because of race, religious or political beliefs, or sexual orientation
prosecute (ˈpros·ĕ·kyoot) *v.* 1. to bring a criminal action against. 2. to carry on, continue, practice

prescribe (pri·ˈskrīb) *v.* 1. to issue commands, order something to be done; dictate. 2. to order a medicine or other treatment
proscribe (proh·ˈskrīb) *v.* to prohibit, forbid by law

raise (rayz) *v.* 1. to lift, make higher; put in an upright position 2. to increase in size, quantity, intensity, degree, or strength. *n.* 1. the act of raising or increasing. 2. an increase in salary
raze (rayz) *v.* 1. to level to the ground, demolish completely. 2. to erase, obliterate

team (teem) *v.* to join together so as to form a team. *n.* a group organized to work together; a cooperative unit
teem (teem) *v.* to be full of; to be present in large numbers

waive (wayv) *v.* 1. to give up (a right or claim) voluntarily, relinquish. 2. to refrain from enforcing or insisting upon (a rule, penalty, standard procedure, etc.); dispense with

wave (wayv) *v.* 1. to move up and down or back and forth; undulate. 2. to signal with an up and down or back and forth movement of the hand. *n.* 1. a ridge or swell on the surface of a body of water. 2. a back-and-forth or up-and-down movement, especially of the hand. 3. a surge, rush, or sudden great rise

TIPS AND STRATEGIES

Homonyms and other frequently confused words can be particularly challenging, especially when you have a limited amount of time to prepare for an exam. Here are some specific tips and strategies to help you make the most of your study time.

- Spelling is often the key to distinguishing between commonly confused words. *Meddle*, for example, differs from *mettle* only because it contains the letter *d* instead of *t*. Use this key difference to help you remember the difference in meaning as well. For example, you might remember that *meddle* with a *d* is something you <u>d</u>on't want to do unless you want to annoy others.
- Review, review, review. Use flash cards or other study strategies to review these commonly confused words until you have them memorized. And then review them again.
- *Use* these words. If you use these words in your everyday writing and conversations, you will remember which word has which meaning. Or teach them to someone else. Teaching something to another person is one of the most effective ways to master that material.
- Remember to make the most of your learning style. Use whatever study or memorization techniques work best for you. For example, if you are a visual learner, create pictures that will help you remember word meanings. If you are an auditory learner, rhymes will be more effective.
- Pay attention to details, and use them to help you remember the words and their meanings. The more carefully you read each definition and the closer you look at the spelling of each word, the more likely you are to find a "key" for you to remember the differences between them. For example, *appraise* has the word *praise* in it. You can associate praise with a good evaluation, and *appraise* means to evaluate.

- Use your ears for the commonly confused words that aren't homophones, and use the difference in pronunciation to help you further differentiate between the words.
- Don't forget to use word parts to remember meaning. Both *prescribe* and *proscribe*, for example, have the root *scrib/script*, meaning to write. Then you can remember that *proscribe* is a (written) law that *pro*hibits something.

PRACTICE QUESTIONS

Choose the correct word in the parenthesis to complete each sentence. Circle your choices or write your answers on a separate piece of paper. Then compare your selections to the correct answers at the end of the chapter.

1. Lilin (*alluded/eluded*) to problems with her boss, but she didn't say anything directly.

2. Xiu is coming this afternoon to determine the (*extant/extent*) of the problem.

3. The checks were (*disbursed/dispersed*) this morning.

4. Once again, Luna has come up with an (*ingenious/ingenuous*) solution to the problem.

5. We will (*waive/wave*) the late fee because of your extenuating circumstances.

6. Please (*precede/proceed*) with caution through the construction zone.

7. Reina is in (*eminent/imminent/emanate*) danger and needs our help right away.

8. Jillian met with a lawyer to see if her landlord could be (*persecuted/prosecuted*) for his negligence of her building.

9. It was a grueling six-hour (*ascent/assent*) from our camp to the top of the mountain.

10. Here is a list of the books the school librarian would like to (*censor/censure/sensor*) because she feels they are inappropriate for children.

ANSWERS

How did you do on identifying the correct word? Check your answers here, and then analyze the results to figure out your plan of attack for mastering this topic.

1. **alluded**. To *allude* means to make an indirect reference to.
2. **extent**. *Extent* means the range, distance, or degree to which something reaches or extends.
3. **disbursed**. To *disburse* means to pay out.
4. **ingenious**. *Ingenious* means marked by inventive skill or creativity; showing inventiveness and skill, remarkably clever.
5. **waive**. To *waive* is to give up (a right or claim) voluntarily, relinquish; to refrain from enforcing or insisting upon (a rule, penalty, standard procedure, etc.).
6. **proceed**. To *proceed* means to go forward or onward, especially after an interruption; move on, advance.
7. **imminent**. *Imminent* means about to occur, impending.
8. **prosecuted**. To *prosecute* is to bring a criminal action against someone.
9. **ascent**. An *ascent* is an upward slope; a movement upward, advancement.
10. **censor**. To *censor* is to forbid the publication, distribution, or other public dissemination of something because it is considered obscene or otherwise politically or morally unacceptable.

Idioms and Vocabulary Variations

Sometimes you will hear English expressions that sound familiar but are hard to define outside of the context in which they are used. They're called **idioms**. Although they don't always follow the general rules of word usage, they are an integral part of any language and are important for you to know.

An idiom can sometimes mean one of a number of things, depending on how it's used within a sentence. In its simplest form, an idiom is an everyday term or expression whose meaning evolved over time as it was used in conversation and informal writing. You will get a better idea of what idioms are by looking at these examples:

➡ I was *tied up* at the office until late last night.
➡ He was *on the phone* when I got to his house.
➡ The candidate's *spin doctors* were on hand to offer comment on the campaign.

Taken literally, these sentences bring to mind peculiar pictures of people roped to their office chairs, perched on top of telephones, or whirling through hospitals! When you look at them in context, however, you know that the first means that someone was delayed at work, the second, that a man was talking on the phone, and the third, that there were people able to interpret a political office seeker's actions in a favorable light. All of these expressions are idioms.

ON YOUR OWN
CAMPUS-SPEAK

You are likely to encounter certain words on a college campus or in any post-high-school program. Some of the words you'll find in the world of academia, or the world of education, might also appear on the TOEFL iBT. These include:

- **tenure:** protected employment for professors who have reached a certain level of rank or experience. A related term is *tenure track,* which means that the position carries with it the possibility of tenure.
- **prerequisite:** requirements needed before a promotion or the granting of a job. In college, the word (sometimes shortened to *prereq*) refers to the course or courses that you must take in order to qualify for an advanced course.
- **semester:** one of two terms in an academic year
- **bursar:** the financial officer of a college
- **tuition:** the cost of attending courses

On your own, try and locate the definitions of the following words, which are frequently heard around campus.

syllabus	transcript	master's degree
practicum	core curriculum	credit
alumni	liberal arts	sabbatical
registrar	elective	dormitory

You might want to use the Internet to locate these definitions, or even ask a university representative.

The word *idiom* is from the Latin word *idio,* referring to the self. An *idiosyncrasy,* for example, is a habit or custom peculiar to one's self. An idiom is seen as any kind of language use that has gained wide usage in that particular language. An idiom is peculiar not to an individual person but to an individual culture's use of language. Here are some things to keep in mind about idioms:

➡ Idioms can be confused with clichés, colloquialisms, and slang.
- **Clichés** are overused phrases that have remained in the language for a long time. "Pretty as a picture," "right as rain," and "selling like hotcakes" are examples of clichés. They are *too* well known to English speakers. Through overuse, their impact is lessened.

- **Colloquialisms** are expressions that may be appropriate in informal speech but are incorrect in formal writing. The use of "should of" for "should have" and "plan on going" instead of "planning to go" are examples of colloquialisms.
- **Slang** is informal language that is often peculiar to a particular age or occupational group. Examples of slang are "tellin' it like it is" or "What's up?"

➡ Idiomatic phrases in English include hundreds of verbs paired with smaller words (prepositions) that change the meaning of the verb. *Watching out for* (being alert to) something is different than *watching over* (attending to) something. You might *get up* early one morning so you can *get away* on a vacation to France, where you hope to *get by* with your high school French so you can *get along* with the locals.

➡ All languages have their own idioms, which can make translation from one language to another a bit difficult. Even different cultures that speak the same language can have trouble understanding each other's idioms. For instance, people in the United Kingdom use idioms that are different from those used in the United States. What people in the United States call an "apartment building," the British call a "block of flats."

 DEFINITION

cliché: an overused word or phrase that has lost its impact in the language; it is a French word used in English

Some idioms are derived from images rooted in experience; it makes sense that *cool heels* would refer to excessive waiting because, presumably, hot heels result from running hard. You could see that *laughing off* something would have to do with not taking it very seriously.

Then there are idioms that have evolved over a long period of time and have no particular logic or origin: for example, *up to the job*. Somewhere in between are idioms whose meanings made sense once upon a time but are now lost. *Spitting image* has nothing to do with saliva. It's a corruption of "spit and image," and *spit* simply meant "exact likeness."

Here are some idioms with their definitions.

give it a shot: try for the first time
watch out: be careful
take a stab at: attempt
laugh off: ignore with good humor

hold off: delay

burnout: a point of physical or emotional exhaustion

fly off the handle: to get angry

life of the party: a person who makes things enjoyable for a group of people

cool his heels: wait a long time

be a wash: even out

spitting image: exact likeness

up to the job: capable of doing the work

by and large: as a general rule

give the slip to: escape

once in a blue moon: very seldom

keep your ears open: to stay attuned

all of a sudden: suddenly

boil down: summarize; amount

catch up: to complete something belatedly

drop off: deposit or deliver

find out: discover, learn

have on: wear

keep + *-ing* verb: continue without interruption

jump in: begin or enter eagerly

make up your mind: settle, decide

put off: to hold back to a later time

show up: arrive, appear

sleep on it: delay making a decision until the next day

take place: happen, occur

used to + verb: something accomplished in the past, but not in the present

HERE'S A HINT
NEW AND EMERGING VOCABULARY

All words have some point of origin. Words that gain sudden popularity in the language often do so because they've grown out of a common new experience or observation. Some of the ways new words are made include:

- shortening longer words—for example, from *gymnasium* to *gym*
- making up acronyms—such as *snafu,* which means "an error" and derives from the phrase "situation normal, all fouled up."
- blending two words together—as in *camcorder* from **camera** and *recorder*
- adapting people's names to ideas that are associated with them—for example, *Reaganomics,* from **Reagan** and *economics.*

TIPS AND STRATEGIES

Idioms and vocabulary variations are likely to appear on standardized tests like TOEFL iBT and occur regularly in newspaper articles, textbooks, and other day-to-day communications. Here are some specific tips and strategies to use as you add these words to your vocabulary and prepare for your exam.

- Use the context of the sentences provided with the definitions to help you understand these words and memorize their meanings.
- Solidify these words and phrases in your memory by teaching them to someone else.
- Pronounce these words each time you go over their meaning. The more you hear how they sound, the more familiar they will feel to you, and the easier it will be to remember them.
- Once again, use the power of mnemonic devices and associations to help you remember meaning.

PRACTICE QUESTIONS

On the lines provided or on a separate piece of paper, indicate whether each of the following expressions represents slang, a colloquialism, or a cliché. Then compare your selection to the correct answers at the end of the chapter.

1. "She *may of* gone to the movies" is an example of _____.

2. "The car battery was *dead as a doornail*" is an example of _____.

3. *Hang a right* at the next corner" is an example of _____.

Answer yes or no to the following sentences, on the basis of your knowledge of the idioms. Then compare your selection to the correct answers at the end of the chapter.

4. If you *burn out* at something, it means that you need the services of an electrician. _____

5. If it happens *once in a blue moon*, it happens rarely. _____

6. If you *give the slip* to someone, you hand over your undergarment. _____

7. You have to stand near a window if you are going to *watch out* for something. _____

8. If you *give something a shot*, you are willing to try. _____

ANSWERS

How did you do on identifying idioms and word variations? Check your answers here, and then analyze the results to figure out your plan of attack for mastering this topic.

1. colloquialism
2. cliché
3. slang
4. no
5. yes
6. no
7. no
8. yes

Practice Test 1

The 80 questions in this practice test will help you assess your vocabulary skills and the topics reviewed throughout this book.

Take your time when answering each question. (We suggest not timing yourself.) Attempt to answer the questions without using a reference tool like a dictionary; however, if you come across words that you are unsure of, make a list of these words. After you complete the test, look up the definitions for the words on your list. It might be a good idea to write down the definition beside the word.

When you are finished, check the answer key carefully to assess your results. Then, you can determine how much time you need to spend to increase your vocabulary power.

Directions: For questions 1 through 20, choose the word that best fills in the blank.

1. George developed an _____ plan to earn the extra money he needed to start his own business.
   a. elitist
   b. irrational
   c. aloof
   d. ingenious

2. We knew everything about the newest member of our group; she was very _____.
   a. expressive
   b. secretive
   c. reserved
   d. artistic

3. I have always liked your positive attitude; it has _____ affected our working relationship.
   a. adversely
   b. shamelessly
   c. candidly
   d. favorably

4. Dog-sitting for Buddy is easy to do; he is a _____ and obedient pet.
   a. delectable
   b. commonplace
   c. meddlesome
   d. docile

5. The directions to the new office were _____, and I had no trouble finding it in time for work.
   a. priceless
   b. arduous
   c. explicit
   d. embodied

6. If your drinking water is not _____, it could cause serious health problems.
   a. valid
   b. quenchable
   c. impure
   d. potable

7. The new board member said she would vote in favor of the proposed city ordinance because it _____ many of the points discussed earlier this year.
   a. encompassed
   b. released
   c. reminisced
   d. dispersed

8. Rachel _____ a plan to become a millionaire by age 30.
   a. conformed
   b. devised
   c. decreased
   d. condoned

9. Wanting to make a good impression, he found himself in a _____ about the right tie to wear to the business meeting.
   a. prestige
   b. redundancy
   c. quandary
   d. deficit

10. Because Mark needed to pass the exam, he made studying a _____ over watching his favorite television show.
    a. priority
    b. conformity
    c. perplexity
    d. concept

11. Hoping to win a prize for the best costume, Tim dressed _____ with bright red suspenders and a purple tie.
    a. eminently
    b. virtuously
    c. conspicuously
    d. obscurely

12. Muhammad fell asleep during the movie because it had a very _____ plot.
    a. monotonous
    b. torrid
    c. ample
    d. vital

13. To get the promotion she wanted, she _____ that it was best to go back to school to get her master's degree as soon as she could.
    a. supposed
    b. surmised
    c. presumed
    d. resolved

14. The narrator's description was an accurate _____ of a true southern family.
    a. portrayal
    b. council
    c. disguise
    d. reunion

15. Due to slippery road conditions and the slope of the narrow, winding highway, the car _____ down the steep mountainous road.
    a. dissented
    b. ventilated
    c. careened
    d. agitated

16. The fire alarm _____ beckoned the volunteer firefighters of the small community to come to action.
    a. approvingly
    b. significantly
    c. symbolically
    d. audibly

17. After running an early 5K race, Simone _____ devoured a hearty breakfast.
    a. dynamically
    b. voraciously
    c. generously
    d. beneficially

18. The car rental company considered the scratches on the driver's door to be caused by a minor _____.
    a. mishap
    b. attraction
    c. reflex
    d. duplicate

19. The participants in the road rally agreed to _____ near the village commons at 5:00.
    a. rendezvous
    b. scatter
    c. filibuster
    d. disperse

20. Understanding the world economic conditions, the recent graduates spoke _____ about job prospects for the future.
    a. warily
    b. luxuriously
    c. measurably
    d. narrowly

Directions: For questions 21 through 45, choose the best definition for the word in italics.

21. Aswad has such a *caustic* sense of humor that most people find his jokes upsetting rather than humorous.
    Caustic means
    a. bitingly sarcastic.
    b. relentlessly funny.
    c. refreshingly honest.
    d. original, cutting edge.

22. Sandra is truly an *enigma;* although she's lived here for years and everyone knows her, no one seems to know anything about who she is or where she came from. *Enigma* means
    a. stranger.
    b. enemy.
    c. newcomer.
    d. mystery.

23. *Exorbitant* means
    a. belonging to a group.
    b. to orbit.
    c. in a new location.
    d. far beyond what is normal or reasonable; very high.

24. *Denunciation* means
   a. to denounce or openly condemn.
   b. critical, of or like a condemnation.
   c. one who denounces or openly condemns another.
   d. the act of denouncing or openly condemning.

25. *Metamorphosis* means
   a. to transform.
   b. one who has changed.
   c. a transformation.
   d. tending to change frequently.

26. To *reconcile* means
   a. to reestablish a close relationship between.
   b. to move away from.
   c. to undermine.
   d. to surpass, outdo.

27. *Didactic* means
   a. a teacher or instructor.
   b. intended to instruct, moralizing.
   c. to preach, moralize.
   d. the process of instructing.

28. *Unilateral* means
   a. to multiply.
   b. understated.
   c. literal.
   d. one-sided.

29. *Subordinate* means
   a. under someone else's authority or control.
   b. organized according to rank, hierarchical.
   c. something ordinary or average, without distinction.
   d. repeated frequently to aid memorization.

30. *Incisive* means
   a. insight.
   b. worthy of consideration.
   c. penetrating, biting in nature.
   d. to act forcefully.

31. *Intermittent* means
   a. badly handled.
   b. occurring at intervals between two times or points.
   c. greatly varied.
   d. a number between one and ten.

32. *Miscreant* means
   a. someone who is unconventional.
   b. someone who lacks creativity.
   c. a very naïve person.
   d. an evil person, villain.

33. *Perennial* means
   a. lasting a very long time, constant.
   b. one who plants a garden.
   c. to establish contact.
   d. the process of encoding a message.

34. *Imperialism* means
   a. one who acquires items from other empires.
   b. an empire built by acquiring other territories.
   c. relating to the acquisition of territories.
   d. the policy of extending an empire by acquiring other territories.

35. To *abrogate* is to
   a. abolish, revoke.
   b. fight, quarrel.
   c. rest quietly.
   d. know intimately.

36. An *acrimonious* relationship is one that
 a. has existed for a long time.
 b. is extremely friendly.
 c. exists only in the imagination.
 d. is bitter or resentful.

37. A *vicarious* action is one that
 a. is experienced through the life or action of another.
 b. enables a guilty person to be set free.
 c. surrenders the rights of others.
 d. has a pleasing and lasting effect on others.

38. If there is *amity* between two nations, there is
 a. war.
 b. equality.
 c. bitterness.
 d. peace.

39. An *edict* is
 a. a place to rest.
 b. a place to stop.
 c. the act of seeing or shining.
 d. a formal proclamation or command.

40. A *magnanimous* person is
 a. highly noble, generous.
 b. extremely talkative.
 c. given to wordy, rambling speech.
 d. a wanderer, hobo.

41. To *acquiesce* is to
 a. call attention to.
 b. speak in a whisper.
 c. mask the truth.
 d. give in to, comply with another's wishes.

42. A *pugnacious* person is best described as
   a. nosy.
   b. combative.
   c. talented.
   d. ruthless.

43. Something that is *erratic*
   a. moves at a constant, steady pace.
   b. is properly ordered; appropriate, in its proper place.
   c. seems to be harmless but is actually very dangerous.
   d. is unpredictable, meandering, straying from the norm.

44. To feel *fervor* is to feel
   a. carefree, light-hearted.
   b. burdened, as with guilt.
   c. intense, fiery emotion.
   d. calmness, peace.

45. A *loquacious* person
   a. has good intentions, but often ends up doing things that end up hurting others.
   b. tends to talk a great deal.
   c. often has difficulty finding things.
   d. tends to like everyone; is not discerning.

Directions: For questions 46 through 59, choose the correct word in the parentheses to complete the sentence.

46. The pond was (*teaming/teeming*) with tadpoles after the frog eggs hatched.

47. Anita's (*faux/foe*) mink coat looked so real that a group of teenagers accused her of cruelty to animals.

48. Jackson may act as if he is totally (*disinterested/uninterested*) in you, but believe me, he is very anxious to learn more about you.

49. I am having the jewelry I inherited from my grandmother (*appraised/apprised*) to find out how much it is worth.

50. Helen entered the room right on (*cue/queue*).

51. You are sure to be (*censored/censured/sensored*) if you make such wild accusations about your colleagues.

52. I have always admired Don's (*meddle/mettle*); he seems to be afraid of no one and nothing.

53. A (*hoard/horde*) of angry parents attended the school board meeting and demanded that the superintendent step down.

54. The documentary really (*peaked/peeked/piqued*) my interest in the Civil War.

55. With just a few hours to go before the big ceremony, Adele rushed around (*prescribing/proscribing*) orders left and right.

56. Huang decided to (*raise/raze*) the stakes by increasing the reward.

57. Although Oscar's story sounds (*incredible/incredulous*), I think he's telling the truth.

58. Jing-Mae gave her (*ascent/assent*) to the proposal, even though she did not entirely agree with the plan.

59. This looks like a (*decent/descent/dissent*) restaurant; let's eat here.

Directions: In questions 60 through 63, identify the correct synonym by looking for word roots, prefixes, or suffixes. Choose the word that means the same or about the same as the italicized word.

60. a *partial* report
    a. identifiable
    b. incomplete
    c. visible
    d. enhanced

61. a *substantial* report
   a. inconclusive
   b. weighty
   c. proven
   d. alleged

62. *corroborate* the statement
   a. confirm
   b. negate
   c. deny
   d. challenge

63. *manufactured* goods
   a. reverted
   b. transgressed
   c. regressed
   d. processed

Directions: In questions 64 through 67, choose the word that means the opposite of the italicized word.

64. *prompt* payment
   a. punctual
   b. slack
   c. tardy
   d. regular

65. rain *delay*
   a. slow
   b. hasten
   c. pause
   d. desist

66. *moderate* work flow
   a. original
   b. average
   c. final
   d. excessive

67. *initial* impression
   a. first
   b. crisis
   c. final
   d. right

Directions: For questions 68 through 72, choose the word whose definition best matches the description.

68. an innovative play that uses an experimental style
   a. apropos
   b. mélange
   c. avant-garde
   d. imbroglio

69. the complete works of Shakespeare
   a. blasé
   b. milieu
   c. zeitgeist
   d. oeuvre

70. a meeting at 7:00 at La Grange restaurant
   a. par excellence
   b. rendezvous
   c. savoir faire
   d. façade

71. "work like a dog," "sleep like a baby," and other such overused sayings
   a. cliché
   b. bourgeois
   c. insouciant
   d. gauche

72. an avid sports fan
   a. gestalt
   b. hiatus
   c. mélange
   d. aficionado

Directions: For questions 73 and 74, choose the word that best describes the section of the word in bold type.

73. **pro**active
    a. after
    b. forward
    c. toward
    d. behind

74. in**scribe**
    a. confine
    b. see
    c. perform
    d. write

75. A synonym for *vast* is
    a. attentive.
    b. immense.
    c. steady.
    d. slight.

76. A synonym for *enthusiastic* is
    a. adamant.
    b. available.
    c. cheerful.
    d. eager.

77. A synonym for *adequate* is
    a. sufficient.
    b. mediocre.
    c. proficient.
    d. average.

78. A synonym for *comply* is
    a. subdue.
    b. entertain.
    c. flatter.
    d. obey.

79. An antonym for *uniform* is
   a. dissembling.
   b. diverse.
   c. bizarre.
   d. slovenly.

80. A synonym for *ecstatic* is
   a. inconsistent.
   b. positive.
   c. wild.
   d. thrilled.

ANSWERS

1. **d.** *Ingenious* means marked by originality, resourcefulness, and cleverness in conception.
2. **a.** An *expressive* person would be one who is open or emphatic when revealing opinions or feelings.
3. **d.** *Favorably* means gracious, kindly, or obliging.
4. **d.** *Docile* means easily led or managed.
5. **c.** *Explicit* means clearly defined.
6. **d.** *Potable* means fit for drinking.
7. **a.** *Encompassed* in this context means included.
8. **b.** *Devised* means to form—in the mind—new combinations or applications of ideas or principles; to plan to obtain or bring about.
9. **c.** *Quandary* means a state of perplexity or doubt.
10. **a.** *Priority* means the right to receive attention before others.
11. **c.** *Conspicuously* means obvious to the eye or mind; attracting attention.
12. **a.** *Monotonous* means having a tedious sameness.
13. **d.** *Resolved* means having reached a firm decision about something.
14. **a.** *Portrayal* means a representation or portrait.
15. **c.** *Careen* means to rush headlong or carelessly; to lurch or swerve while in motion.
16. **d.** *Audibly* means heard or the manner of being heard.
17. **b.** *Voraciously* means having a huge appetite; ravenously.
18. **a.** A *mishap* is an unfortunate accident.
19. **a.** A *rendezvous* is a meeting or assembly that is by appointment or arrangement.

20. **a.** *Warily* is a manner marked by keen caution, cunning, and watchful prudence.

21. **a.** *Caustic* means bitingly sarcastic, cutting; able to burn or dissolve by chemical action. The main context clue is that people find Aswad's jokes upsetting rather than humorous; thus choice **a** is the only option that makes sense.

22. **d.** *Enigma* means something that is puzzling or difficult to understand; a baffling problem or riddle. The context tells you that people know who Sandra is, but no one knows anything about her; thus, she remains a mystery.

23. **d.** The prefix *ex-* means out, out of, away from. *Exorbitant* means greatly exceeding (far away from) the bounds of what is normal or reasonable.

24. **d.** The noun suffix *-tion* means the act or state of. *Denunciation* means the act of denouncing, especially in public; to openly condemn or accuse of evil.

25. **c.** The noun suffix *-sis* means the process of. *Metamorphosis* means a transformation, a marked change of form, character, or function. Choices **b** and **c** are both nouns, but for choice **b** to be correct, it would require the suffix *-ist*.

26. **a.** The prefix *re-* means back, again. To *reconcile* means to reestablish a close relationship between, to bring back to harmony.

27. **b.** The adjective suffix *-ic* means pertaining or relating to, having the quality of. *Didactic* means intended to instruct; tending to be excessively instructive or moralizing. Only choice **b** defines a quality.

28. **d.** The prefix *uni-* means one. *Unilateral* means one-sided. Notice also the adjective suffix *-al*, meaning action or process.

29. **a.** The prefix *sub-* means under, beneath, below. The adjective *subordinate* means (1) of a lower or inferior class or rank; secondary; (2) subject to the authority or control of another. As a noun it means one that is subordinate to another, and as a verb (notice the *-ate* suffix) it means (1) to put in a lower or inferior rank or class; (2) to make subservient; subdue.

30. **c.** The adjective suffix *-ive* means having the nature of. *Incisive* means penetrating and clear; sharp, acute, biting.

31. **b.** The prefix *inter-* means between or among. *Intermittent* means occurring at intervals, not continuous; periodic, alternate.

32. **d.** The prefix *mis-* means bad, evil, wrong. *Miscreant* means a villain, criminal; an evil person.

33. **a.** The adjective suffix *-ial* means having the quality of, related to, suitable for. *Perennial* means lasting an indefinitely long time, forever; constantly recurring, happening again and again or year after year. Choice **a** is the only adjective definition.

34. **d.** The noun suffix *-ism* means state or doctrine of. *Imperialism* means the policy of extending rule of a nation or empire by acquiring other territories.

35. **a.** The root *rog* means to ask. The prefix *ab-* means off, away from, away, down; the suffix *-ate* means to make, cause to be. To *abrogate* means to abolish, do away with, formally revoke.

36. **d.** The root *ac/acr* means sharp, bitter. The adjective suffix *-ous* means having the quality of or relating to. *Acrimonious* means bitter and sharp in language or tone.

37. **a.** The root *vi* means life. The adjective suffix *-ous* means having the quality of or relating to. *Vicarious* means felt through imaging what another has experienced; acting or suffering for another.

38. **d.** The root *am* means love. The noun suffix *-ity* means state of being. *Amity* means friendship; a state of friendly or peaceful relations.

39. **d.** The root *dic/dict/dit* means to say, tell, use words. An *edict* is an official order or decree; a formal proclamation or command issued by someone in authority.

40. **a.** The root *mag/maj/max* means big. The adjective suffix *-ous* means having the quality of or relating to. *Magnanimous* means very noble and generous; understanding and forgiving of others.

41. **d.** The root *qui* means quiet. To *acquiesce* means to comply, give in, consent without protest—thereby "quieting" the other to whom one gives in.

42. **b.** The root *pug* means to fight. The adjective suffix *-ous* means having the quality of or relating to. *Pugnacious* means quarrelsome, combative, inclined to fight.

43. **d.** The root *err* means to wander. The adjective suffix *-ic* means pertaining or relating to, having the quality of. *Erratic* means moving or behaving in an irregular, uneven, or inconsistent manner; deviating (wandering) from the normal or typical course of action, opinion, etc.

44. **c.** The root *ferv* means to boil, bubble, burn. The suffix *-or* means a condition or activity. *Fervor* means zeal, ardor, intense emotion.

45. **b.** The root *loc/log/loqu* means word, speech. The adjective suffix *-ous* means having the quality of or relating to. *Loquacious* means very talkative, garrulous.

46. **teeming.** To *teem* means to be full of, to be present in large numbers.

47. **faux.** *Faux* means artificial, fake; not genuine or real.

48. **uninterested.** *Uninterested* means not interested, having no care or interest in knowing.

49. **appraised.** To *appraise* means to evaluate, to establish value or estimate the worth of.

50. **cue.** A *cue* is a signal, such as a word or action, given to prompt or remind someone of something; a hint or suggestion.

51. **censured.** To *censure* is to criticize strongly, rebuke, condemn.

52. **mettle.** *Mettle* means courage, fortitude, spirit.

53. **horde.** A *horde* is a large group or crowd, a vast multitude.

54. **piqued.** To *pique* is (1) to cause annoyance or irritation, to vex; (2) to provoke or arouse. This sentence uses the second meaning.

55. **prescribing.** To *prescribe* is to issue commands, order something to be done, dictate. It also means to order a medicine or other treatment.

56. **raise.** To *raise* is to lift, make higher; to increase in size, quantity, intensity, degree, or strength.

57. **incredible.** *Incredible* means implausible, beyond belief; astonishing.

58. **assent.** *Assent* means agreement, concurrence, consent.

59. **decent.** *Decent* means (1) conforming to what is socially or morally suitable or correct; (2) meeting acceptable standards, sufficient, adequate. This sentence uses the second meaning.

60. **b.** *Partial* means *incomplete*. The root of the word here is *part*. A partial report is only part of the whole.

61. **b.** A *substantial* report is extensive. The key part of the word substantial is *substance*. Substance means something that has significance.

62. **a.** To *corroborate* is *confirm*. Notice the prefix *co-*, which means with or together. Some related words are *cooperate*, *coworker*, and *collide*. Corroboration means that one statement fits with another.

63. **d.** *Manufactured* goods are those that are made or processed from raw material into a finished product. *Facer*—the word root—means to make or do.

64. **c.** The key here is to remember not to choose the synonym. Context clues are important as well. You may have seen this sentence on one of your bills: *Prompt payment is appreciated. Prompt* means punctual; *tardy* means late.

65. **b.** A delay is a postponement in time. If you rely on context clues to help you answer this question, you may be reminded of a rain delay at a sporting event. To *delay* is to slow; to *hasten* is to hurry.

66. **d.** Something that is moderate is not subject to extremes. *Moderate* means average; *excessive* means extreme.

67. **c.** An initial impression is one that comes first. *Initial* means first; *final* means last.

68. **c.** *Avant-garde* means using or favoring an ultramodern or experimental style; innovative, cutting-edge, especially in the arts or literature.

69. **d.** *Oeuvre* means (1) a work of art; (2) the total lifework of a writer, artist, composer, etc.

70. b. The noun *rendezvous* means (1) a prearranged meeting at a certain time and place; (2) a place where people meet, especially a popular gathering place. The verb *rendezvous* means to bring or come together at a certain place, to meet at a rendezvous.

71. a. A *cliché* is a trite or overused expression or idea.

72. d. An *aficionado* is a fan or devotee, especially of a sport or pastime.

73. b. The prefix *pro* means for. If someone is *proactive*, they are forward thinking and take action or initiative to make things happen.

74. d. The word root *scribe* means to write; to engrave on a surface.

75. b. *Vast* means very great in size; *immense*.

76. d. *Enthusiastic* means eager.

77. a. If something is *adequate*, it is sufficient.

78. d. *Comply* is synonymous with obey.

79. b. To be *uniform* is be consistent or the same as others; to be *diverse* is to have variety.

80. d. A person who is *ecstatic* is *thrilled*.

Practice Test 2

The 80 questions in this practice test will help you assess your vocabulary skills and the topics reviewed throughout this book.

Take your time when answering each question. (We suggest not timing yourself.) Attempt to answer the questions without using a reference tool like a dictionary; however, if you come across words that you are unsure of, make a list of these words. After you complete the test, look up the definitions for the words on your list. It might be a good idea to write down the definition beside the word.

When you are finished, check the answer key carefully to assess your results. Then, you can determine how much time you need to spend to increase your vocabulary power.

Directions: For questions 1 through 18, choose the word that best fills in the blank.

1. Being a direct relative of the deceased, her claim to the estate was
   _____.
   a. optional
   b. vicious
   c. prominent
   d. legitimate

2. The hail _____ the cornfield until the entire crop was lost.
   a. belittled
   b. pummeled
   c. rebuked
   d. commended

3. The Earth Day committee leader placed large garbage bins in the park to
   _____ Saturday's cleanup.
   a. confound
   b. pacify
   c. integrate
   d. facilitate

4. Her rapport with everyone in the office _____ the kind of inter-personal skills that all of the employees appreciated.
   a. prevailed
   b. diverged
   c. exemplified
   d. varied

5. The _____ of the two rivers provided the perfect place to build a new state park.
   a. assumption
   b. confluence
   c. seclusion
   d. treatise

6. Do you have the _____ paperwork you need to register for the class?
   a. punitive
   b. grandiose
   c. restorative
   d. requisite

7. Do not _____ yourself; you must pass the last exam of the semester to graduate.
   a. delude
   b. depreciate
   c. relinquish
   d. prohibit

8. When you address the members of the committee, be sure to give a _____ description of the new office procedures.
   a. principled
   b. determined
   c. comprehensive
   d. massive

9. Although Hunter was _____ about revealing information to us
   when we first met him, he soon began to talk more than anyone.
   a. customary
   b. reticent
   c. animated
   d. voluntary

10. The darkening skies in the west were a _____ to the dangerous
    thunderstorm that summer afternoon.
    a. tedium
    b. precursor
    c. preference
    d. momentum

11. The news was no longer secret; Martin Kemp _____ told the press
    that he had accepted the nomination as board chairperson.
    a. repulsively
    b. reputedly
    c. perpetually
    d. principally

12. After an hour of heavy rain, the thunderstorm _____, and we were
    able to continue our golf game.
    a. abated
    b. germinated
    c. constricted
    d. evoked

13. After years of experience, Florin became a _____ veterinarian who
    could treat and operate on many different kinds of animals.
    a. acute
    b. superficial
    c. consummate
    d. ample

14. Anthony, a meticulous young man, _____ watered his neighbors'
plants once a week while they were on vacation.
   a. terminally
   b. perpendicularly
   c. diligently
   d. haphazardly

15. _____ elephants from the wild not only endangers the species but
upsets the balance of nature.
   a. Irritating
   b. Poaching
   c. Provoking
   d. Smuggling

16. The two cats could be _____ only by the number of rings on their
tails; otherwise, they were exactly alike.
   a. separated
   b. divided
   c. disconnected
   d. differentiated

17. On each slick curve in the road, I was afraid we would _____ and
have an accident.
   a. operate
   b. hydroplane
   c. submerge
   d. reconnoiter

18. My cousin claimed to be _____; evidently she was right because
she always seemed to know what would happen in the future.
   a. dreamlike
   b. comical
   c. criminal
   d. clairvoyant

Directions: For questions 19 through 45, choose the best definition for the word in italics.

19. Although the plot of the film is admittedly *trite*, the characters are so endearing that the movie is highly entertaining despite the old storyline. *Trite* means
    a. original.
    b. exciting.
    c. complex.
    d. overused.

20. Ilka has always *emulated* her older brother, so it is no surprise that she is also pursuing a career as a neuroscientist. To *emulate* means
    a. to support wholeheartedly.
    b. to strive to equal, imitate, or outdo.
    c. to be more successful than.
    d. to regard as inferior.

21. Everyone loved Ilona's idea, and she quickly *garnered* enough support for her proposal to present it to the committee. To *garner* means
    a. to create.
    b. to propose.
    c. to demonstrate.
    d. to withhold.

22. Cy's attempt to finally complete the marathon was *thwarted* when he twisted his ankle in the 23rd mile. To *thwart* means
    a. to injure seriously.
    b. to prevent from accomplishing.
    c. to support actively.
    d. to be excessively competitive.

23. To *subjugate* means
    a. to be the subject of a sentence or conversation.
    b. to conquer, bring under control.
    c. to be wrongly or unevenly distributed.
    d. to be surrounded on all sides.

24. *Benevolence* means
    a. kindness, generosity.
    b. a kind, generous ruler.
    c. to be generous with one's time or money.
    d. kind, giving charitably.

25. To *coalesce* means
    a. to dig up, mine.
    b. to carry out an ill-conceived or poorly planned course of action.
    c. to combine and form a whole; join together.
    d. to withdraw silently, especially in shame.

26. *Docile* means
    a. one who domesticates animals.
    b. the management of domestic affairs.
    c. obedience.
    d. willing to obey, easily managed or taught.

27. *Anomaly* means
    a. regularity, consistency.
    b. something that is irregular, abnormal, or deviates from the usual form.
    c. a surprising collaboration, the cooperation of unlikely individuals.
    d. discontent among a specific group within a larger population.

28. *Lamentable* means
    a. regrettable, unfortunate.
    b. to regret.
    c. an unfortunate occurrence.
    d. to do something regrettable.

29. To *abscond* means
    a. to create a secret hiding place.
    b. to do something without telling anyone.
    c. to go away secretly and hide.
    d. to do something ahead of deadline.

30. *Disparate* means
    a. chosen from within.
    b. exceeding expectations.
    c. from the same origin.
    d. fundamentally different, distinct, or apart from others.

31. *Rectify* means
    a. to correct.
    b. a correction.
    c. a surprising error.
    d. an editor.

32. *Inscrutable* means
    a. teaching a lesson.
    b. having little or no impact.
    c. kept between or within members of a family.
    d. not fathomable; incapable of being understood.

33. *Antipathy* means
    a. that which occurred previously.
    b. a strong aversion or dislike.
    c. an examination of all aspects of an issue.
    d. the act of separating from the source.

34. *Neophyte* means
    a. original, unique.
    b. something that comes from multiple sources.
    c. a roommate; someone who lives with another.
    d. a beginner or novice.

35. A *belligerent* person is
    a. from another country, foreign.
    b. kind, eager to help.
    c. eager to fight, hostile.
    d. loving, devoted.

36. Someone who is *omniscient*
    a. often speaks without thinking.
    b. receives the maximum benefit.
    c. blames others for his or her own faults.
    d. is eager to please.

37. A *renaissance* is
    a. a rebirth.
    b. a punishment.
    c. a lie.
    d. a mistake.

38. To *equivocate* is to
    a. burn or sting.
    b. speak in a way that conceals the truth.
    c. put something in its proper place.
    d. calm or quiet.

39. Something that is *manifest* is
    a. everywhere.
    b. newborn.
    c. obvious.
    d. deadly.

40. Something that is *luminous* is
    a. bright, shining.
    b. even, equal.
    c. excessive.
    d. full of knowledge.

41. A person who is *culpable* is
    a. capable.
    b. vocal.
    c. energetic, full of life.
    d. guilty.

42. Something that is *innocuous* is
  a. dangerous or deadly.
  b. irrelevant, wandering from the main path or point.
  c. harmless, inoffensive.
  d. clean, thoroughly washed.

43. To *juxtapose* is to
  a. place side by side.
  b. overwhelm, flood.
  c. be born again.
  d. speak in a round-about manner.

44. Someone who is *reticent* is
  a. fair, judging equally.
  b. reserved, silent.
  c. bubbling over with enthusiasm.
  d. deeply in love.

45. A *veritable* autograph is
  a. very valuable.
  b. an autograph by a famous person.
  c. genuine.
  d. a forgery or fake.

Directions: For questions 46 through 59, choose the correct word in the parentheses to complete the sentence.

46. I tried everything, but nothing would (*elicit/illicit*) a response from the child.

47. The Euro has (*deprecated/depreciated*), but the dollar is up.

48. Stop (*persecuting/prosecuting*) me just because I often disagree with you.

49. Tomorrow the city is going to (*raise/raze*) the building that I grew up in.

50. As soon as I get off the phone, I will (*appraise/apprise*) you of the situation.

51. The odor quickly (*disbursed/dispersed*) through the room, and soon it was no longer even noticeable.

52. I don't like Igor because he is constantly (*meddling/mettling*) in things that are none of his business.

53. Although you all seem to agree, I must (*decent/descent/dissent*); I think this is a bad decision.

54. Dixie is so (*ingenious/ingenuous*) I don't think she could lie if her life depended on it.

55. I'm just going to (*peak/peek/pique*) in the baby's room to make sure she's okay.

56. The thief managed to (*allude/elude*) the police for several days, but they finally caught up with him in Reno.

57. The (*cue/queue*) for the movies was all the way to the end of the block and around the corner.

58. Georgio had to (*fain/feign*) excitement when he opened his presents so his parents wouldn't know he'd already searched their room to find out what he was getting.

59. A strange odor is (*eminenting/imminenting/emanating*) from Professor Van Buren's laboratory.

Directions: In questions 60 through 63, identify the correct synonym by looking for word roots, prefixes, or suffixes. Choose the word that means the same or about the same as the italicized word.

60. an *incoherent* answer
   a. not understandable
   b. not likely
   c. undeniable
   d. challenging

61. covered with *debris*
    a. good excuses
    b. transparent material
    c. scattered rubble
    d. protective material

62. *inadvertently* left
    a. mistakenly
    b. purposely
    c. cautiously
    d. carefully

63. *compatible* workers
    a. gifted
    b. competitive
    c. harmonious
    d. experienced

Directions: In questions 64 through 67, choose the word that means the opposite of the italicized word.

64. *capable* employee
    a. unskilled
    b. absurd
    c. apt
    d. able

65. *zealous* pursuit
    a. envious
    b. eager
    c. idle
    d. comical

66. *exorbitant* prices
    a. expensive
    b. unexpected
    c. reasonable
    d. outrageous

67. *belligerent* attitude
    a. hostile
    b. appeasing
    c. instinctive
    d. ungracious

Directions: For questions 68 through 72, choose the word whose definition best matches the description.

68. an artist's first gallery showing
    a. ennui
    b. imbroglio
    c. parvenu
    d. debut

69. a temporary separation in a relationship
    a. blasé
    b. quid pro quo
    c. hiatus
    d. malaise

70. wearing a disguise
    a. incognito
    b. imbroglio
    c. milieu
    d. oeuvre

71. pretending not to be hurt by an insulting remark
    a. ad hoc
    b. gauche
    c. cliché
    d. façade

72. someone who reports students' questions and concerns to the dean
    a. aficionado
    b. liaison
    c. parvenu
    d. vis-à-vis

Directions: For questions 73 and 74, choose the word or phrase that best describes the section of the word in bold type.

73. **con**gregation
    a. with
    b. over
    c. apart
    d. time

74. wis**dom**
    a. a state of being
    b. a relationship
    c. a property
    d. an action

75. A synonym for *affect* is
    a. accomplish.
    b. cause.
    c. sicken.
    d. influence.

76. An antonym for *wary* is
    a. alert.
    b. leery.
    c. worried.
    d. careless.

77. An antonym for *novel* is
    a. dangerous.
    b. unsettled.
    c. suitable
    d. old.

78. A synonym for *continuous* is
    a. intermittent.
    b. adjacent.
    c. uninterrupted.
    d. contiguous.

79. A synonym for *courtesy* is
   a. civility.
   b. congruity.
   c. conviviality.
   d. rudeness.

80. An antonym for *fallacy* is
   a. truth.
   b. blessing.
   c. weakness.
   d. fable.

ANSWERS

1. **d.** *Legitimate* means in a manner conforming to recognized principles or accepted rules or standards.
2. **b.** *Pummeled* means to pound or beat.
3. **d.** *Facilitate* means to make easier or help bring about.
4. **c.** *Exemplify* means to be an instance of or serve as an example.
5. **b.** *Confluence* means a coming or flowing together, a meeting, or a gathering at one point.
6. **d.** *Requisite* means essential or necessary.
7. **a.** *Delude* means to mislead the mind; to deceive.
8. **c.** *Comprehensive* means covering completely or broadly.
9. **b.** *Reticent* means inclined to be silent or uncommunicative, reserved.
10. **b.** *Precursor* means something that comes before.
11. **d.** *Reputedly* means according to general belief.
12. **a.** *Abated* means to decrease in force or intensity.
13. **c.** *Consummate* means extremely skilled and experienced.
14. **c.** *Diligently* means to do something with careful attention and great effort.
15. **b.** To *poach* is to trespass on another's property in order to steal fish or game.
16. **d.** To *differentiate* between two things is to establish the distinction between them.
17. **b.** When a car goes out of control and skims along the surface of a wet road, it is called *hydroplaning*.
18. **d.** A *clairvoyant* is someone who can perceive matters beyond the range of ordinary perception.

19. **d.** *Trite* means repeated too often, overly familiar through overuse. The key context clue is the phrase "the old storyline," which indicates that the plot of the movie is overused.

20. **b.** To *emulate* means to try to equal or excel, especially by imitation. The sentence tells you that Ilka is pursuing the same career as her brother, which indicates that she is trying to equal or outdo him through imitation.

21. **d.** To *garner* means to gather, amass, or acquire. The sentence tells you that Ilona quickly found the support she needed to present her idea to the committee; also because the sentence states that people loved Ilona's idea, it is logical to conclude that she would gather their support.

22. **b.** To *thwart* means to prevent the accomplishment or realization of something. Cy's twisted ankle kept him from realizing his attempt to complete the marathon.

23. **b.** The prefix *sub-* means under or below. To *subjugate* means to conquer, subdue, bring under control. Notice also the verb suffix *-ate*, meaning one that performs, promotes, or causes an action; being in a specified state or condition.

24. **a.** The noun suffix *-ence* means state of. *Benevolence* means the inclination to be kind and generous; a disposition to act charitably.

25. **c.** The prefix *co-* means with, together. *Coalesce* means to combine and form a whole; to join together, fuse.

26. **d.** The adjective suffix *-ile* means having the qualities of. *Docile* means willing to obey, ready and willing to be taught, or easily managed.

27. **b.** The prefix *a-* mean not, without. *Anomaly* means something that deviates from the general rule or usual form; one that is irregular or abnormal.

28. **a.** The adjective suffix *-able* means capable or worthy of. *Lamentable* means regrettable, unfortunate; inspiring grief or mourning.

29. **c.** The prefix *ab-* means off, away from, apart, down. To *abscond* means to go away secretly and hide oneself, especially after wrongdoing.

30. **d.** The prefix *dis-* means away from, apart, reversal, not. *Disparate* means fundamentally different or distinct; dissimilar, varied.

31. **a.** The verb suffix *-ify* means to make. To *rectify* means to make right, correct.

32. **d.** The prefix *in-* means not. *Inscrutable* means baffling, unfathomable, incapable of being understood. Notice also the adjective suffix *-able*.

33. **b.** The prefix *anti-* means against, opposed to. *Antipathy* means a strong aversion or dislike.

34. **d.** The prefix *neo-* means new, recent, a new form of. *Neophyte* means a beginner or novice.

35. **c.** The root *bel* means war. The ending *-ent* is an adjective suffix meaning in a state or condition; performing or causing a specified action. *Belligerent* means hostile and aggressive, showing an eagerness to fight.

36. **d.** The root *omni* means all; the root *sci* means to know. *Omniscient* means having infinite knowledge, knowing all things.

37. **a.** The root *nas/nat/nai* means to be born. The prefix *re-* means back or again; the suffix *-ance* means state of. *Renaissance* means a rebirth or revival.

38. **b.** The root *equ* means equal; the root *voc/vok* means to call; the suffix *-ate* means to make, cause to be. To *equivocate* means to use unclear or ambiguous language in order to mislead or conceal the truth. Thus, someone who equivocates is "equally" lying and telling the truth (or rather, not quite doing either).

39. **c.** The root *man* means hand. *Manifest* means clear and unmistakable, obvious; thus, at hand. The correct answer can be achieved here through the process of elimination, as the other answers correspond with different roots.

40. **a.** The root *luc/lum/lus* means light; the suffix *-ous* means having the quality of or relating to. *Luminous* means shining, emitting light; full of light, brilliant.

41. **d.** The root *culp* means blame. The adjective suffix *-able* means capable or worthy of. *Culpable* means deserving blame or censure for doing something wrong or harmful; blameworthy, guilty.

42. **a.** The root *nec/nic/noc/nox* means harm, death. The prefix *in-* means not; the suffix *-ous* means having the quality of or relating to. Thus, *innocuous* means harmless, having no adverse or ill effects.

43. **a.** The root *pon/pos/pound* means to put, place. To *juxtapose* means to place side by side, especially to compare or contrast.

44. **b.** The root *tac/tic* means to be silent. *Reticent* means tending to keep one's thoughts and feelings to oneself; reserved, untalkative, silent.

45. **c.** The root *ver* means truth. The suffix *-able* means capable or worthy of. *Veritable* means real, true, genuine.

46. **elicit.** To *elicit* means (1) to call forth or draw out, to provoke; (2) to deduce or derive by reasoning. This sentence uses the first meaning.

47. **depreciated.** To *depreciate* means to diminish in price or value, to lessen the worth of. It also means to think or speak of as being of little worth, to belittle.

48. **persecuting.** To *persecute* is to oppress, harass, or mistreat, especially because of race, religious or political beliefs, or sexual orientation.

49. **raze**. To *raze* is (1) to level to the ground, demolish completely; (2) to erase, obliterate. This sentence uses the first meaning.

50. **apprise**. To *apprise* means to give notice or information to, to make aware of, inform.

51. **dispersed**. To *disperse* is (1) to separate and scatter in different directions, or cause to do so; (2) to distribute widely, disseminate. This sentence uses the first meaning.

52. **meddling**. To *meddle* is to intrude in other people's affairs, interfere.

53. **dissent**. To *dissent* is (1) to differ in opinion, disagree; (2) to withhold approval or assent. This sentence uses the first meaning.

54. **ingenuous**. *Ingenuous* means (1) not cunning or deceitful, unable to mask feelings; artless, frank sincere; (2) lacking sophistication or worldliness. This sentence uses the first meaning.

55. **peek**. To *peek* is to glance quickly or peer at furtively.

56. **elude**. To *elude* is (1) to escape from or evade, especially by cleverness, daring, or skill; (2) to be incomprehensible to, escape the understanding of.

57. **queue**. A *queue* is (1) a line of waiting people or vehicles; (2) in information processing, an ordered list of tasks to be performed or sequence of programs awaiting processing. This sentence uses the first meaning.

58. **feign**. To *feign* is to pretend, to give the false appearance of.

59. **emanating**. To *emanate* is to come or issue forth, as from a source.

60. **a.** *Incoherent* means not understandable. To *cohere* means to connect. A coherent answer connects or makes sense. The prefix *in-* means not.

61. **c.** *Debris* is scattered fragments or trash.

62. **a.** *Inadvertently* means by mistake. The key element in this word is the prefix *in-*, which means not.

63. **c.** *Compatible* means capable of existing or performing in harmony.

64. **a.** The suffix *-able* tells you that a capable employee is one who has ability. *Capable* means able; *unskilled* means unable.

65. **c.** *Zealous* means eager, so *idle* is most nearly the opposite. You may have heard the word *zeal* before, which might give you a clue about the meaning of the word. One other precaution is to be careful and not be misled by the similar sounds of *zealous* and *jealous*. The other trick is not to choose the synonym, *eager*; choice **b.**

66. **c.** The best clue in this word is the prefix *ex-*, which means out of or away from. *Exorbitant* literally means exceeding the bounds of what is fair or normal; very high. The opposite of an *exorbitant* or *outrageous* price would be a *reasonable* one.

67. **b.** The key element in this word is the root *belli*, which means warlike. The synonym choices—*hostile* and *ungracious*—would be incorrect. The antonym would be *appeasing*.

68. **d.** A *debut* is a first appearance in or presentation to the public.

69. **c.** *Hiatus* means a gap or opening; an interruption or break.

70. **a.** *Incognito* means with one's identity concealed; in disguise or under an assumed character or identity.

71. **d.** A *façade* is (1) the face or front of a building; (2) an artificial or deceptive front, especially one intended to hide something unpleasant.

72. **b.** *Liaison* means (1) a channel or means of connection or communication between two groups; one who maintains such communication; (2) a close relationship or link, especially one that is secretive or adulterous.

73. **a.** The prefix *con-* means to be together with. A *congregation* would gather together with each other in a house of worship.

74. **a.** The suffix *-dom* is a state of being. Someone who has *wisdom* is someone who is wise enough to discern or judge what is right, true, or lasting.

75. **d.** To *affect* means to influence.

76. **d.** To be *wary* is to be on guard or watchful; *careless* is the opposite of watchful.

77. **d.** To be *novel* is to be new; the opposite is *old*.

78. **c.** *Continuous* means marked by *uninterrupted* extension in space and time.

79. **a.** A *courtesy* is a courteous or mannerly act; it is characterized by *civility*.

80. **a.** A *fallacy* is a false or mistaken idea, trickery; a *truth* is something that conforms to the facts.

Word List

By now you've seen that a good working vocabulary is a very important asset when taking the TOEFL iBT. Remember that the best way to learn vocabulary is also the easiest: make long lists of words you don't know and then break them down into short lists. Learn a short list every day.

You should also try and write sentences using the new words. When you learn a new word, use it in conversation as soon as possible. Repetition is key—use a word three times, and it's yours!

Another alternative is to work with flash cards. Flash cards are pieces of paper or index cards that are used as a learning aid. Write the vocabulary word on one side and the definition on the other. Or, try writing a sentence that uses the word on one side of the flash card and the definition of the word on the other. Flash cards are easy to handle, they're portable, and they're friend-friendly, so you can study with a buddy. You and your friends can drill each other. If you can make games out of learning vocabulary, studying will be more fun and you will learn more as well!

Now, review the word list. After each vocabulary word, you will find the word's pronunciation, part of speech, definition, and a sentence using the word. (Note: Some words have different meanings depending on how they are being used.) If the word list looks intimidating, try the following strategy.

1. Figure out how many days there are until you take the TOEFL iBT.
2. Multiply that number by 10.

If you have only 30 days until the test day, you can learn 300 new words, by studying only ten new words each day! And, remember, some of these words may already be familiar to you.

PRONUNCIATION KEY

Before you review the word list, here a list of the pronunciation symbols used in the definitions. Next to each pronunciation symbol are words chosen to illustrate how the symbols are said aloud. You may want to photocopy the next few pages so that you will be able to refer to this list easily.

a	hat, carry, fact	ng	sing, finger, frank
ă	ago, dependable, pedal	o	odd, fox, trot
ah	palm, father	ŏ	salmon, advisor
ahr	car, chart, farm	oh	oak, boat, sew
air	bare, scare, fair	ohr	aboard, score, coarse
aw	ball, walk, draw	oi	oil, coin, coy
ay	stage, blame, day	oo	ooze, noodle, super
b	bat, rabbit, crib	oor	pour, cure, sure
ch	church, preacher	or	for, scorn, horse
d	day, puddle, bed	ow	out, house, how
e	egg, head, cherry	p	pan, paper, pop
ě	shaken, trickle	r	rain, marry, dear
ee	eat, treat, tree	s	sun, listen, rice
eer	ear, clear, cheer	sh	share, fishing, cash
f	fan, stuffy, relief	t	tip, mutter, pot
g	go, regular, fog	th	three, strengthen, breath
h	heed, heaven, unhappy	*th*	this, father, breathe
hw	whether, nowhere	u	cup, come, shut
i	it, live, middle	ŭ	delicious, measure
ĭ	stencil, edible	ur	her, turn, worry
ī	icy, tire, sky	uu	cook, put, pull
j	jug, tragic, hedge	v	vail, sliver, live
k	kitten, shaken, track	w	want, aware, quaint
l	lost, trolley, toll	y	you, yarn, yesterday
m	more, summon, slim	z	zebra, hazy, please
n	no, dinner, man	zh	division, treasure

WORD LIST

A

abate (ă·'bayt) *v.* to lessen in strength, intensity, or degree; subside. *As the violent storm abated, we began to survey the damage it caused.*

aberration (ăb·ĕ·'ray·shŏn) *n.* deviation from what is normal, distortion. *His new scientific theory was deemed an aberration by his very conservative colleagues.*

abeyance (ă·'bay·ăns) *n.* suspension, being temporarily suspended or set aside. *Construction of the highway is in abeyance until we get agency approval.*

abhor (ab·'hohr) *v.* to regard with horror or repugnance, detest. *I know Carlos abhors politics, but he should still get out and vote.*

abjure (ab·'joor) *v.* 1. to repudiate, renounce under oath. 2. to give up or reject. *When Joseph became a citizen, he had to abjure his allegiance to his country of origin.*

abrogate ('ab·rŏ·gayt) *v.* to abolish, do away with, formally revoke. *The dictator abrogated agreements that no longer suited his purposes.*

abscond (ab·'skond) *v.* to go away secretly and hide oneself, especially after wrongdoing to avoid prosecution. *He threw down his gun and absconded from the scene of the crime.*

absolution (ab·sŏ·'loo·shŏn) *n.* 1. an absolving or clearing from blame or guilt. 2. a formal declaration of forgiveness, redemption. *The jury granted Alan the absolution he deserved.*

abstain (ab·'stayn) *v.* 1. to choose to refrain from an action or practice. 2. to refrain from voting. *I have decided to abstain on this issue.*

abstemious (ab·'stee·mee·ŭs) *adj.* 1. using or consuming sparingly; used with temperance or moderation. 2. eating and drinking in moderation; sparing in the indulgence of appetites or passions. *After Vadeem gained 30 pounds, he decided he needed a more abstemious diet.*

abstruse (ab·'stroos) *adj.* difficult to comprehend, obscure. *Albert Einstein's abstruse calculations can be understood by only a few people.*

abysmal (ă·'biz·măl) *adj.* 1. extreme, limitless, profound. 2. extremely bad. *It was not surprising that the movie was a flop; the reviews were abysmal.*

accolade ('ak·ŏ·layd) *n.* 1. praise or approval. 2. a ceremonial embrace in greeting. 3. a ceremonious tap on the shoulder with a sword to mark the conferring of knighthood. *He received accolades from his superiors for finding ways to cut costs and increase productivity.*

accretion (ă·'kree·shŏn) *n.* 1. growth or increase by gradual, successive addition; building up. 2. (in biology) the growing together of parts that are normally separate. *The accretion of sediment in the harbor channel caused boats to run aground.*

acquiesce (ak·wee·'es) *v.* to comply, give in, consent without protest. *After the police officer explained why the street was closed to pedestrian traffic, I acquiesced and walked to the next street.*

acrid ('ak·rid) *adj.* 1. having an unpleasantly bitter, sharp taste or smell. 2. bitter or caustic in language or manner. *The burning tires in the junkyard gave off an acrid odor.*

acrimonious (ak·rĭ·'moh·nee·ŭs) *adj.* bitter and sharp in language or tone. *Jasleen did not like her new neighbors; it was obvious in the acrimonious way she spoke to them.*

acumen (ă·'kyoo·mĕn) *n.* quickness, keenness, and accuracy of perception, judgment, or insight. *With Jonelle's acumen, she would make an excellent trial lawyer.*

ad hoc (ad 'hok) *adj.* for a specific, often temporary, purpose; for this case only. *An ad hoc committee will be formed to investigate Stella's allegations.*

adamant ('ad·ă·mănt) *adj.* 1. unyielding to requests, appeals, or reason. 2. firm, inflexible. *The senator was adamant that no changes would be made to the defense budget.*

addle ('ad·ĕl) *v.* 1. to muddle or confuse. 2. to become rotten, as in an egg. *The prosecuting attorney's questions addled the defendant.*

ado (ă·'doo) *n.* fuss, trouble, bother. *Without much ado, she completed her book report.*

adroit (ă·'droit) *adj.* skillful, clever, or adept in action or in thought; dexterous, deft. *Priya is a very adroit seamstress; she should have your trousers fixed in no time.*

agrarian (ă·'grair·ee·ăn) *adj.* relating to or concerning land and its ownership or cultivation. *Although his family tried to convince him to move to a big city, Greg preferred his agrarian life as a farmer.*

aficionado (ă·fish·yo·'nah·doh) *n.* a fan or devotee, especially of a sport or pastime. *Sal is such an Rolling Stones aficionado that he bought tickets to all ten Giants Stadium concerts.*

alacrity (ă·'lak·ri·tee) *n.* a cheerful willingness; being happily ready and eager. *The alacrity she brought to her job helped her move up the corporate ladder quickly.*

allay (ă·ˈlay) *v.* 1. to reduce the intensity of, alleviate. 2. to calm, put to rest. *The remarks by the CEO did not allay the concerns of the employees.*

allude (ă·ˈlood) *v.* to make an indirect reference to. *The presidential candidate alluded to the recent unemployment problem by saying, "We've all made sacrifices."*

altercation (awl·tĕr·ˈkay·shŏn) *n.* a heated dispute or quarrel. *To prevent an altercation at social functions, one should avoid discussing politics and religion.*

amiable (ˈay·mee·ă·bĕl) *adj.* friendly and agreeable; good natured, likable, pleasing. *Miguel was usually the first person invited to a party; his amiable personality drew people to him.*

amity (ˈam·ĭ·tee) *n.* friendship; a state of friendly or peaceful relations. *Amity had existed between Denise and Suzanne since they decided not to fight about money anymore.*

ambivalent (am·ˈbiv·ă·lĕnt) *adj.* having mixed or conflicting feelings about a person, thing, or situation; uncertain. *She was ambivalent about the proposal for the shopping center because she understood both the arguments for and against its construction.*

ameliorate (ă·ˈmeel·yŏ·rayt) *v.* to make or become better, to improve. *The diplomat was able to ameliorate the tense situation between the two nations.*

amorphous (ă·ˈmor·fŭs) *adj.* 1. having no definite form or distinct shape; shapeless. 2. of no particular kind or character, anomalous. *Andrea looked up at the sky, looking at the amorphous clouds.*

amulet (ˈam·yŭ·lit) *n.* something worn around the neck as a charm against evil. *The princess wore an amulet after being cursed by a wizard.*

anachronism (ă·ˈnak·rŏ·niz·ĕm) *n.* 1. something that is placed into an incorrect historical period. 2. a person, custom, or idea that is out of date. *With the rise in popularity of cell phones, pagers seem like an anachronism.*

anarchy (ˈan·ăr·kee) *n.* 1. the complete absence of government or control resulting in lawlessness. 2. political disorder and confusion. *After the king's assassination, the country fell into a state of anarchy.*

anomaly (ă·ˈnom·ă·lee) *n.* something that deviates from the general rule or usual form; one that is irregular, peculiar, or abnormal. *Everyone in my family enjoys seafood, so my uncle's distaste for the salmon dish was an anomaly.*

antagonist (an·ˈtag·ŏ·nist) *n.* one who opposes or contends with another; an adversary, opponent. *Hillary was Mike's antagonist as they both competed for the lead role in the play.*

antecedent (an·ti·'see·dĕnt) *n.* that which precedes; the thing, circumstance, event that came before. *The police are trying to determine the antecedent of the deadly car crash.*

anthropomorphic (an·thrŏ·pŏ·'mor·fik) *adj.* attributing human characteristics, motivations, or behavior to animals or inanimate objects. *Many mythologies are about anthropomorphic deities, who express human characteristics such as love, envy, and sadness.*

antipathy (an·'tip·ă·thee) *n.* 1. a strong aversion or dislike. 2. an object of aversion. *After Inti stole Peter's wallet, Peter had antipathy for his classmate.*

antithesis (an·'tith·ĕ·sis) *n.* the direct or exact opposite, opposition or contrast. *Martin's parenting style is the antithesis of mine; he is strict, I am not.*

apathetic (ap·ă·'thet·ik) *adj.* feeling or showing a lack of interest, concern, or emotion; indifferent, unresponsive. *Many students were apathetic when the principal resigned after thirty years working at the school.*

aperture ('ap·ĕr·chŭr) *n.* an opening or gap, especially one that lets in light. *The aperture setting on a camera has to be set perfectly to ensure that pictures will have enough light.*

apex ('ay·peks) *n.* 1. the highest point. 2. tip, pointed end. *Upon reaching the apex of the mountain, the climbers placed their flag in the snow.*

apocalypse (ă·'pok·ă·lips) *n.* a cataclysmic event bringing about total devastation or the end of the world. *Many people feared an apocalypse would immediately follow the development of nuclear weapons.*

apostate (ă·'pos·tayt) *n.* one who abandons long-held religious or political convictions. *Disillusioned with religious life, Reverend Gift lost his faith and left the ministry, not caring if he'd be seen as an apostate by colleagues who chose to remain.*

apotheosis (ă·poth·ee·'oh·sis) *n.* deification, an exalted or glorified ideal. *Hanson was so in love with Marge; in his daydreams, she was an apotheosis.*

appease (ă·'peez) *v.* to make calm or quiet, soothe; to still or pacify. *The only way to appease Lawrence is to concede that he is right.*

appraise (ă·'prayz) *v.* 1. to evaluate. 2. to establish value or estimate the worth of. *The art dealer appraised the value of the painting.*

apprise (ă·'prīz) *v.* to give notice or information to; to make aware of, inform. *The teacher apprised the class about when the midterm and final exams would occur.*

approbation (ap·rŏ·ˈbay·shŏn) *n.* approval. *The local authorities issued an approbation to close the street for a festival on St. Patrick's Day.*

appropriate (ă·ˈprŏ·prē·ĭt) *adj.* suitable for a particular person, condition, occasion, or place; fitting. (ă·ˈproh·pree·ayt) *v.* to take for one's own use, often without permission; to set aside for a special purpose. *The state legislature will appropriate two million dollars from the annual budget to build a new bridge on the interstate highway.*

apropos (ap·rŏ·ˈpoh) *adj.* appropriate to the situation; suitable to what is being said or done. *adv.* 1. by the way, incidentally. 2. at an appropriate or opportune time. *Chancey's comments may have been disturbing, but they were definitely apropos.*

arcane (ahr·ˈkayn) *adj.* mysterious, secret, beyond comprehension. *A number of college students in the 1980s became involved in the arcane game known as "Dungeons and Dragons."*

archaic (ahr·ˈkay·ik) *adj.* belonging to former or ancient times; characteristic of the past. *The archaic language of Chaucer's tales makes them difficult for many students to understand.*

archetype (ˈahr·ki·tīp) *n.* an original model from which others are copied; original pattern or prototype. *Elvis Presley served as the archetype for rock and roll performers in the 1950s.*

ardor (ˈahr·dŏr) *n.* fiery intensity of feeling; passionate enthusiasm, zeal. *The ardor Larry brought to the campaign made him a natural spokesperson.*

arduous (ˈahr·joo·ŭs) *adj.* 1. very difficult, laborious; requiring great effort. 2. difficult to traverse or surmount. *Commander Shackleton's arduous journey through the Arctic has become the subject of many books and movies.*

ascent (ă·ˈsent) *n.* 1. an upward slope. 2. a movement upward, advancement. *The rock climbers made the ascent up the side of the mountain.*

ascetic (ă·ˈset·ik) *adj.* practicing self-denial, not allowing oneself pleasures or luxuries; austere. *Some religions require their leaders to lead an ascetic lifestyle as an example to their followers.*

askew (ă·ˈskyoo) *adj. & adv.* crooked, not straight or level; to one side. *Even the pictures on the wall stood askew after my five-year-old son's birthday party.*

asperity (ă·ˈsper·i·tee) *n.* harshness, severity; roughness of manner, ill temper, irritability. *The asperity that Marvin, the grumpy accountant, brought to the meetings usually resulted in an early adjournment.*

assay (ă·'say) *v.* 1. to try, put to a test. 2. to examine. 3. to judge critically, evaluate after an analysis. *The chief engineer wanted a laboratory to assay the steel before using it in the construction project.*

assent (ă·'sent) *n.* agreement; concurrence; consent. *v.* to agree to something especially after thoughtful consideration. *In order to pass the new law, the committee must reach an assent.*

assiduous (ă·'sij·oo·ŭs) *adj.* diligent, hardworking; persevering, unremitting. *Omar's teachers applaud his assiduous study habits.*

assuage (ă·'swayj) *v.* to make something less severe, to soothe; to satisfy (as hunger or thirst). *The small cups of water offered to the marathon runners helped to assuage their thirst.*

attenuate (ă·'ten·yoo·ayt) *v.* 1. to make thin or slender. 2. to weaken, reduce in force, value, or degree. *The Russian army was able to attenuate the strength and number of the German forces by leading them inland during winter.*

audacious (aw·'day·sh ŭs) *adj.* fearlessly or recklessly daring or bold; unrestrained by convention or propriety. *Detective Malloy's methods were considered bold and audacious by his superiors, but they often achieved results.*

augment (awg·'ment) *v.* to increase in size, strength, or intensity; enlarge. *Arty tried to help Ann and Stan settle their differences, but his interference only augmented the problem.*

august (aw·'gust) *adj.* majestic, venerable; inspiring admiration or reverence. *Jackie Kennedy's august dignity in the days following her husband's assassination set a tone for the rest of the nation as it mourned.*

auspice ('aw·spis) *n.* 1. protection or support, patronage. 2. a forecast or omen. *The children's art museum was able to continue operating through the auspices of an anonymous wealthy benefactor.*

austere (aw·'steer) *adj.* 1. severe or stern in attitude or appearance. 2. simple, unadorned, very plain. *I know my dad seems austere, but he's really just a great big teddy bear.*

authoritarian (ă·thor·i·'tair·i·ăn) *adj.* favoring complete, unquestioning obedience to authority as opposed to individual freedom. *The military maintains an authoritarian environment for its officers and enlisted men alike.*

automaton (aw·'tom·ă·tŏn) *n.* someone who acts or responds in a mechanical or robotic way. 2. a self-operating or automatic machine, a robot. *Because she fol-*

lowed the same routine every morning, Natasha made coffee, cooked breakfast, and made her children's lunch like an automaton.

autonomy (aw·'ton·ŏ·mee) *n.* personal or political independence; self-government, self-determination. *The teenager desired fewer rules from her parents and a sense of autonomy.*

avant-garde (a·vahnt·'gahrd) *adj.* using or favoring an ultramodern or experimental style; innovative, cutting-edge, especially in the arts or literature. *Yvette prefers the avant-garde style of writers like Donald Barthelme to the traditional narrative technique.*

aversion (ă·'vur·zhŏn) *n.* 1. a strong, intense dislike; repugnance. 2. the object of this feeling. *Todd has an aversion to arugula and picks it out of his salads.*

B

baleful ('bayl·fŭl) *adj.* harmful, menacing, destructive, sinister. *Whether it's a man, woman, car, or animal, you can be certain to find at least one baleful character in a Stephen King horror novel.*

balk (bawk) *v.* 1. to stop abruptly and refuse to go on. 2. to obstinately refuse or oppose. *Old man Jones was finally ready to capitulate and sell his land to the timber company, but he balked when he saw that he would be compensated for only half of the value of his property.*

banal (bă·'nal) *adj.* commonplace, trite; obvious and uninteresting. *I was expecting something original and exciting, but the film turned out to have a banal storyline and mediocre acting.*

bane (bayn) *n.* 1. cause of trouble, misery, distress, or harm. 2. poison. *The bane of the oak tree is the Asian beetle.*

beguile (bi·'gīl) *v.* to deceive or cheat through cunning; to distract the attention of, divert; to pass time in a pleasant manner, to amuse or charm. *Violet was able to beguile the spy, causing him to miss his secret meeting.*

belie (bi·'lī) *v.* 1. to give a false impression, misrepresent. 2. to show to be false, to contradict. *By wearing an expensive suit and watch, Alan hoped to belie his lack of success to everyone at the reunion.*

bellicose ('bel·ĭ·kohs) *adj.* belligerent, quarrelsome, eager to make war. *There was little hope for peace following the election of a candidate known for his bellicose nature.*

belligerent (bi·ˈlij·ĕr·ĕnt) *adj.* hostile and aggressive, showing an eagerness to fight. *Because Omar had a reputation for being belligerent, many people refused to associate with him because they feared confrontation.*

benevolence (bĕ·ˈnev·ŏ·lĕns) *n.* the inclination to be kind and generous; a disposition to act charitably. *Regina showed benevolence when she volunteered to help raise money for the local soup kitchen.*

benign (bi·ˈnīn) *adj.* 1. gentle, mild, kind; having a beneficial or favorable nature or influence. 2. not harmful or malignant. *Simo's actions toward his competitors was never mean-spirited; he always acted in a benign manner.*

bevy (ˈbev·ee) *n.* 1. a large group or assemblage. 2. a flock of animals or birds. *There was a bevy of eager bingo fans waiting outside the hall for the game to begin.*

bilk (bilk) *v.* to deceive or defraud; to swindle, cheat, especially to evade paying one's debts. *The stockbroker was led away in handcuffs, accused of trying to bilk senior citizens out of their investment dollars.*

blasé (blah·ˈzay) *adj.* 1. uninterested because of frequent exposure or indulgence. 2. nonchalant, unconcerned. 3. very sophisticated. *Quincy has traveled so much that he speaks of exotic places such as Borneo in a totally blasé manner.*

blasphemy (ˈblas·fĕ·mee) *n.* contemptuous or irreverent acts, utterances, attitudes or writings against God or other things considered sacred; disrespect of something sacrosanct. *If you committed blasphemy during the Inquisition, you would be tortured and killed.*

blatant (ˈblay·tant) *adj.* completely obvious, not attempting to conceal in any way. *Samuel's blatant disregard of the rules earned him a two-week suspension.*

blight (blīt) *n.* 1. a plant disease that causes the affected parts to wilt and die. 2. something that causes this condition, such as air pollution. 3. something that impairs or destroys. 4. an unsightly object or area. *They still do not know what caused the blight that destroyed half of the trees in the orchard.*

blithe (blīth) *adj.* light-hearted, casual, and carefree. *Rachel's blithe attitude toward spending money left her broke and in debt.*

boisterous (ˈboi·stĕ·rŭs) *adj.* 1. loud, noisy, and lacking restraint or discipline. 2. stormy and rough. *The boisterous crowd began throwing cups onto the field during the football game.*

bolster (ˈbohl·stĕr) *v.* 1. to support or prop up. 2. to buoy or hearten. *Coach Edmond's speech bolstered the team's confidence.*

bombastic (bom·'bas·tik) *adj.* speaking pompously, with inflated self-importance. *Ahmed was shocked that a renowned and admired humanitarian could give such a bombastic keynote address.*

boor (boor) *n.* a crude, offensive, ill-mannered person. *Seeing Chuck wipe his mouth with his sleeve, Maribel realized she was attending her senior prom with a classic boor.*

bourgeois (boor·'zhwah) *adj.* typical of the middle class; conforming to the standards and conventions of the middle class; hence also, commonplace, conservative, or materialistic. *Although she won millions in the lottery, Ada still maintains her bourgeois lifestyle.*

bowdlerize ('bohd·lě·rīz) *v.* to edit by omitting or modifying parts that may be considered offensive; censor. *To make their collection of fairy tales suitable for children, the Brothers Grimm had to bowdlerize the folk tales they had collected, for many of the original tales included graphic language.*

bravado (bră·'vah·doh) *n.* false courage, a show of pretended bravery. *Kyle's bravado often got him in trouble with other kids in the neighborhood.*

broach (brohch) *v.* 1. to bring up, introduce, in order to begin a discussion of. 2. to tap or pierce, as in to draw off liquid. *It was hard for Sarah to broach the subject of her mother's weight gain.*

bumptious ('bump·shŭs) *adj.* arrogant, conceited. *The bumptious man couldn't stop talking about himself or looking in the mirror.*

buoyant ('boi·ănt) *adj.* 1. able to float. 2. light-hearted, cheerful. *In science class, the children tried to identify which objects on the table would be buoyant.*

burgeon ('bur·jŏn) *v.* to begin to grow and flourish; to begin to sprout, grow new buds, blossom. *The tulip bulbs beneath the soil would burgeon in early spring providing there was no late frost.*

burnish ('bur·nish) *v.* to polish, rub to a shine. *When Kathryn began to burnish the old metal tea pot, she realized that it was, in fact, solid silver.*

C

cabal (kă·'bal) *n.* 1. a scheme or conspiracy. 2. a small group joined in a secret plot. *With Antonio as their leader, the members of the unit readied themselves to begin the cabal.*

cacophony (kă·'kof·ŏ·nee) *n.* loud, jarring, discordant sound; clamor, din. *I heard a cacophony coming from the garage where the band was practicing.*

cadge (kaj) *v.* to beg, to obtain by begging. *Their dog Cleo would cadge at my feet, hoping I would throw him some table scraps.*

cajole (kă·'johl) *v.* to urge with gentle and repeated appeals or flattery; to wheedle. *Valerie is quite adept at cajoling others to get what she wants, even if it's something she hasn't earned.*

candor ('kan·dŏr) *n.* frank, sincere speech; openness. *When I told my boss about my performance concerns, he welcomed my candor.*

capitulate (kă·'pich·ŭ·layt) *v.* to surrender under specific terms or agreed upon conditions; to give in, acquiesce. *Old man Jones was finally ready to capitulate and sell his land to the timber company, but he balked when he saw that he would be compensated for only half of the value of his property.*

capricious (kă·'prish·ŭs) *adj.* impulsive, whimsical and unpredictable. *Robin Williams, the comedian, demonstrates a capricious nature even when he is not performing.*

careen (kă·'reen) *v.* 1. to lurch from side to side while in motion. 2. to rush carelessly or headlong. *Watching the car in front of us careen down the road was very frightening.*

caste (kast) *n.* a distinct social class or system. *While visiting India, Michael was fascinated to learn the particulars of each caste and the way they related to each other.*

castigate ('kas·tĭ·gayt) *v.* to inflict a severe punishment on; to chastise severely. *When his parents caught Bryan stealing money from his classmates, they castigated him.*

catharsis (kă·'thahr·sis) *n.* the act of ridding or cleansing; relieving emotions via the experiences of others, especially through art. *Survivors of war often experience a catharsis when viewing Picasso's painting* Guernica, *which depicts the bombing of a town during the Spanish civil war.*

caustic ('kaws·tik) *adj.* 1. able to burn, corrode, or dissolve by chemical action. 2. bitingly sarcastic, cutting. *The mechanic was very careful when working with the caustic fluid around the car because it could damage the car's paint.*

censor ('sen·sŏr) *n.* an official who reviews books, films, etc. to remove what is considered morally, politically, or otherwise objectionable. *v.* to forbid the publication, distribution, or other public dissemination of something because it is considered obscene or otherwise politically or morally unacceptable. *The librarian served as a censor, deciding what books were appropriate for the young readers.*

censure ('sen·shŭr) *n.* expression of strong criticism or disapproval; a rebuke or condemnation. *v.* to criticize strongly, rebuke, condemn. *After Tyra was found cheating on the exam, her mother censured her behavior.*

chastise ('chas·tīz) *v.* to punish severely, as with a beating; to criticize harshly, rebuke. *Charles knew that his wife would chastise him after he inadvertently told the room full of guests that she had just had a face lift.*

chauvinist ('shoh·vĭn·ist) *n.* a person who believes in the superiority of his or her own kind; an extreme nationalist. *Though common in the early days of the women's movement, male chauvinists are pretty rare today.*

chimera (ki·'meer·ă) *n.* 1. (in Greek mythology) a fire-breathing she-monster with a lion's head, a goat's body, and a serpent's tail. 2. a vain or incongruous fancy; a (monstrous) product of the imagination, illusion. *Seduced by the chimera of immortality, Victor Frankenstein created a monster that ended up destroying him and everyone he loved.*

chronic ('kron·ik) *adj.* 1. continuing for a long time; on-going, habitual. 2. long-lasting or recurrent. *Seamus has had a chronic cough for the past six months.*

chronicle ('kron·i·kĕl) *n.* a detailed record or narrative description of past events. *v.* to record in chronological order; make a historical record. *Historians have made a chronicle of the war's events.*

chronology (krŏ·'nol·ŏ·jee) *n.* the arrangement of events in time; the sequence in which events occur. *The firefighter determined the chronology of incidents that contributed to the fire.*

chronometer (krŏ·'nom·i·tĕr) *n.* an exceptionally accurate clock; a precise instrument for measuring time. *The track coach used a chronometer to determine the runner's time for the marathon.*

churlish ('chur·lĭsh) *adj.* ill-mannered, boorish, rude. *Angelo's churlish remarks made everyone at the table uncomfortable and ill at ease.*

circumspect ('sur·kŭm·spekt) *adj.* cautious, wary, watchful. *The prison guard was circumspect when he learned that some of the prisoners were planning an escape.*

clandestine (klan·'des·tin) *adj.* conducted in secrecy; kept or done in private, often in order to conceal an illicit or improper purpose. *The private investigator followed Raul to a clandestine rendezvous with a woman in sunglasses and a trench coat.*

cliché (klee·'shay) *n.* a trite or overused expression or idea. *Tito has an engaging writing style, but he uses too many clichés.*

coalesce (koh·ă·'les) *v.* to combine and form a whole; to join together, fuse. *Jay and Jael coalesced their money to create one savings account.*

coeval (koh·'ee·văl) *adj.* of the same time period, contemporary. *The poet Ben Jonson was coeval to Shakespeare.*

cogent ('koh·jĕnt) *adj.* convincing, persuasive, compelling belief. *Ella's cogent arguments helped the debate team win the state championship.*

collusion (kŏ·'loo·zhŏn) *n.* a secret agreement between two or more people for a deceitful or fraudulent purpose; conspiracy. *The discovery of the e-mail proved that collusion existed between the CEO and CFO to defraud the shareholders.*

complacent (kŏm·'play·sĕnt) *adj.* contented to a fault; self-satisfied, unconcerned. *Renee was complacent even when she learned that her coworkers were trying to get her fired.*

concede (kŏn·'seed) *v.* 1. to acknowledge or admit as true, proper, etc. (often with reluctance); to yield, surrender. 2. to grant as a right or privilege. *The leader conceded the right to vote to all her country's inhabitants.*

conciliatory (kŏn·'sil·ee·ă·tohr·ee) *adj.* making or willing to make concessions to reconcile, soothe, or comfort; mollifying, appeasing. *Abraham Lincoln made conciliatory gestures toward the South at the end of the Civil War.*

conclave ('kon·klav) *n.* a private or secret meeting. *The double agent had a conclave with the spy he was supposed to be observing.*

consensus (kŏn·'sen·sŭs) *n.* general agreement or accord; an opinion or position reached by a group. *The school board reached a consensus about building a new high school.*

consternation (kon·stĕr·'nay·shŏn) *n.* a feeling of deep, incapacitating horror or dismay. *The look of consternation on the faces of the students taking the history exam alarmed the teacher, who thought he had prepared his students for the test.*

contentious (kŏn·'ten·shŭs) *adj.* 1. quarrelsome, competitive, quick to fight. 2. controversial, causing contention. *With two contentious candidates on hand, it was sure to be a lively debate.*

conundrum (kŏ·'nun·drŭm) *n.* a hard riddle, enigma; a puzzling question or problem. *Alex's logic professor gave the class a conundrum to work on over the weekend.*

copious ('koh·pi·ŭs) *adj.* large in number or quantity; abundant, plentiful. *The shipwrecked couple found a copious supply of coconut trees and shellfish on the island.*

cornucopia (kor·nyŭ·'koh·pi·ă) *n.* abundance; a horn of plenty. *The first-graders made cornucopias for Thanksgiving by placing papier-mache vegetables into a hollowed-out horn.*

corroborate (kŏ·'rob·ŏ·rayt) *v.* to strengthen or support with evidence or authority; to make more certain, confirm. *Both Irma's and Ye's statements corroborate Tia's story, so she must be telling the truth.*

countenance ('kown·tĕ·năns) *n.* the appearance of a person's face, facial features and expression. *As she walked down the aisle, Julia's countenance was absolutely radiant.*

craven ('kray·vĕn) *adj.* cowardly. *"This craven act of violence will not go unpunished," remarked the police chief.*

credulous ('krej·ŭ·lŭs) *adj.* gullible, too willing to believe things. *All the tables, graphs, and charts made the company's assets look too good to the credulous potential investors at the meeting.*

crux (kruks) *n.* the central or critical point or feature, especially of a problem. *The crux of the trial was her whereabouts at the time of the burglary.*

cryptic ('krip·tik) *adj.* having a hidden or secret meaning, mysterious; hidden, secret, occult. *Jimmy was confused by the cryptic note he found written on the refrigerator.*

cue (kyoo) *n.* 1. a signal, such as a word or action, given to prompt or remind someone of something; a hint or suggestion. 2. a line of waiting people or vehicles; a queue. *When the timer buzzed, Sonia realized that it was a cue to take the hamburgers off the grill.*

culpable ('kul·pă·bĕl) *adj.* deserving blame or censure for being or doing something wrong or harmful; blameworthy, guilty. *When my prank ending up breaking Andrea's lamp, I admitted that I was culpable.*

cursory ('kur·sŏ·ree) *adj.* hasty and superficial. *Although I should have proofread the essay carefully, I only had time to give it a cursory review.*

D

daunt (dawnt) *v.* to intimidate, to make afraid or discouraged. *His austere manner daunted the small children.*

debacle (di·'bah·kĕl) *n.* 1. a sudden disaster or collapse; a total defeat or failure. 2. a sudden breaking up or breaking loose; violent flood waters, often caused by the breaking up of ice in a river. *Putting the bridge's supporting beams in loose sand caused a total debacle when the sand shifted and the bridge fell apart.*

debut (day·'byoo) *n.* a first appearance in or presentation to the public. *v.* to make a first appearance in public. *Irina's Carnegie Hall debut received rave reviews.*

decimate ('des·ĭ·mayt) *v.* to destroy a large portion of. *Neglect and time would eventually decimate much of the housing in the inner cities.*

decorum (di·'kohr·ŭm) *n.* appropriateness of behavior, propriety; decency in manners and conduct. *When questions concerning decorum arise, I always refer to Emily Post.*

de facto (dee 'fak·toh) *adj. & adv.* in reality or fact; actual. *The king is only the nominal head of the country; the de facto leader is the prime minister.*

deign (dayn) *v.* to condescend, to be kind or gracious enough to do something thought to be beneath one's dignity. *Would you deign to spare a dime for a poor old beggar like me?*

delineate (di·'lin·ee·ayt) *v.* to draw or outline, sketch; to portray, depict, describe. *The survey will clearly delineate where their property ends.*

delude (di·'lood) *v.* to deceive, make someone believe something that is wrong. *Nicole deluded Maria when she claimed to forgive her.*

demagogue ('dem·ă·gawg) *n.* a leader who obtains power by appealing to people's feelings and prejudices rather than by reasoning. *The dictator was widely regarded as an infamous demagogue.*

demur (di·'mur) *v.* to raise objections, hesitate. *Polly hated to demur, but she didn't think adding ten cloves of garlic to the recipe would taste good.*

demure (di·'myoor) *adj.* modest and shy, or pretending to be so. *When it was to her advantage, Sharon could be very demure, but otherwise she was quite outgoing.*

denigrate ('den·i·grayt) *v.* to blacken the reputation of, disparage, defame. *The movie script reportedly contained scenes that would denigrate the queen, so those scenes were removed.*

denouement (day·noo·'mahn) *n.* the resolution or clearing up of the plot at the end of a narrative; the outcome or solution of an often complex series of events. *The students sat at the edge of their seats as they listened to the denouement of the story.*

deprecate ('dep·rĕ·kayt) *v.* to express disapproval of; to belittle, depreciate. *Grandpa's tendency to deprecate the children's friends was a frequent source of family strife.*

derisive (di·'rī·siv) *adj.* scornful, expressing ridicule; mocking, jeering. *In order to promote freedom of expression, derisive comments were forbidden in the classroom.*

derivative (di·'riv·ă·tiv) *n.* something that is derived or made by derivation. *adj.* derived from another source, unoriginal. *The word "atomic" is a derivative of the word "atom."*

desecrate ('des·ĕ·krayt) *v.* to violate the sacredness of, to profane. *Someone desecrated the local cemetery by spray-painting graffiti on tombstones.*

destitute ('des·ti·toot) *adj.* 1. penniless, extremely poor. 2. utterly lacking. *After the economy declined, many families were left destitute.*

desultory ('des·ŭl·tohr·ee) *adj.* aimless, haphazard; moving from one subject to another without logical connection. *Ichabod's desultory ramblings worsened as his disease progressed.*

detract (di·'trakt) *v.* to draw or take away from; to remove part of something, diminish. *Unfortunately, Helen's slovenly appearance detracted from the impact of her otherwise brilliant presentation.*

dichotomy (dī·'kot·ŏ·mee) *n.* division into two usually contradictory parts or kinds. *When the teacher broached the subject of politics, there was a predictable dichotomy among the students.*

diffident ('dif·i·dĕnt) *adj.* lacking self-confidence, shy and timid. *Alan used to be so diffident, but now he's as gregarious as can be and is usually the life of the party.*

diffuse (di·'fyooz) *v.* 1. to spread throughout, disperse, extend. 2. to soften, make less brilliant. *adj.* 1. spread out, scattered, not concentrated. 2. wordy, verbose. *The perfume she sprayed diffused throughout her bedroom.*

digress (dī·'gres) *v.* to turn aside, deviate, or swerve; to stray from the main subject in writing or speaking. *Her argument digressed from the main problem she had about her friend's spending habits.*

dilatory ('dil·ă·tohr·ee) *adj.* slow or late in doing something; intended to delay, especially to gain time. *Miguel's dilatory approach to getting himself up and dressed was his own small act of passive resistance to having to work on a holiday.*

disabuse (dis·ă·'byooz) *v.* to undeceive, correct a false impression or erroneous belief. *Natalie needed to disabuse Chin of his belief that she was in love with him.*

discern (di·'surn) *v.* to perceive clearly; to distinguish, recognize as being distinct. *Remy discerned that Opal had no intention of calling him back.*

disconcert (dis·kŏn·'surt) *v.* 1. to upset the composure of, ruffle. 2. to frustrate plans by throwing into disorder. *The arrival of Miriam's ex-husband and his new wife managed to disconcert the typically unflappable Miriam.*

disconsolate (dis·'kon·sŏ·lit) *adj.* 1. sad, dejected, disappointed. 2. inconsolable, hopelessly unhappy. *The disconsolate look on Peter's face revealed that the letter contained bad news.*

disdain (dis·'dayn) *n.* a feeling or showing of haughty contempt or scorn; a state of being despised. *v.* 1. to regard with haughty contempt or scorn, despise. 2. to consider or reject (someone or something) as unworthy or beneath one's dignity. *I was humiliated by the way Angelica disdained every idea I proposed at that meeting.*

disenfranchise (dis·en·'fran·chīz) *v.* to deprive of the rights of citizenship, especially the right to vote. *The independent monitors were at polling locations to ensure neither party tried to disenfranchise incoming voters.*

disingenuous (dis·in·'jen·yoo·ŭs) *adj.* 1. insincere, calculating; not straightforward or frank. 2. falsely pretending to be unaware. *Carl's disingenuous comments were not taken seriously by anyone in the room.*

disparage (di·'spar·ij) *v.* to speak of in a slighting or derogatory way, belittle. *Comedians often disparage politicians as part of their comedic routines.*

dissipate ('dis·ĭ·payt) *v.* 1. to separate and scatter completely; to disperse to the point of disappearing, or nearly so. 2. to be extravagant and wasteful, especially in the pursuit of pleasure; squander. *The crowd dissipated when the riot police arrived, and only the very angriest protesters remained.*

dissemble (di·'sem·bĕl) *v.* to disguise or conceal one's true feelings or motives behind a false appearance. *Tom needed to dissemble his goal of taking his boss's job by acting supportive of his boss's planned job change.*

dissuade (di·'swayd) *v.* to discourage from or persuade against a course of action. *I tried to dissuade them from painting their house purple, but they didn't listen.*

dither ('dith·ĕr) *v.* 1. to hesitate, be indecisive and uncertain. 2. to shake or quiver. *During a crisis, it is important to have a leader who will not dither.*

dogma ('dawg·mă) *n.* a system of principles or beliefs, a prescribed doctrine. *Some find the dogma inherent in religion a comfort, whereas others find it too restrictive.*

dormant ('dor·mănt) *adj.* 1. lying asleep or as if asleep, inactive, at rest. 2. inactive but capable of becoming active; latent, temporarily quiescent. *The geology students made a surprising discovery: the volcano believed to be dormant was about to erupt.*

draconian (dray·'koh·ni·ăn) *adj.* very harsh, extremely severe (especially a law or punishment). *Students of international policy are often shocked by the draconian punishments used by other countries for seemingly minor offenses.*

droll (drohl) *adj.* amusing in an odd or whimsical way. *This is a wonderful, droll story—the children will love it!*

dross (draws) *n.* 1. waste product, sludge. 2. something worthless, commonplace, or trivial. *Work crews immediately began the task of cleaning the dross at the abandoned plastics factory.*

dulcet ('dul·sit) *adj.* melodious, harmonious, sweet-sounding. *The chamber orchestra's dulcet tunes were a perfect ending to a great evening.*

dupe (doop) *n.* someone who is easily deceived, gullible. *v.* to deceive, trick. *Charlene was duped into buying this lemon of a car by a slick-talking salesman.*

E

ebb (eb) *n.* the return of the tide to the sea. *v.* 1. to flow back or recede, as the tide. 2. to fall back, decline. *I hope Mark's anger has ebbed; I am eager for a reconciliation.*

ebullient (i·'bul·yĕnt) *adj.* bubbling over with enthusiasm, exuberant. *The ebullient children were waiting to stick their hands into the grab bag and pull out a toy.*

eccentric (ik·'sen·trik) *adj.* deviating from the conventional or established norm or pattern; anomalous, irregular. *Her artwork was unlike any other artist at the museum; each painting had its own eccentric color scheme.*

eclectic (i·'klek·tik) *adj.* 1. selecting or employing elements from a variety of sources, systems, or styles. 2. consisting of elements from a variety of sources. *You're sure to meet someone interesting at the party—Marieka always invites an eclectic group of people to her gatherings.*

éclat (ay·'klah) *n.* conspicuous success; great acclaim or applause; brilliant performance or achievement. *Even the ruinous deceit of the envious Salieri could not impede the dazzling éclat of the young and gifted Mozart.*

edifying ('ed·ĭ·fī·ing) *adj.* enlightening or uplifting with the aim of improving intellectual or moral development; instructing, improving. *His edifying speech challenged the audience to devote more time to charitable causes.*

efficacious (ef·ĭ·'kay·shŭs) *adj.* acting effectively, producing the desired effect or result. *Margaret's efficacious approach to her job in the collections department made her a favorite with the CFO.*

effrontery (i·'frun·tĕ·ree) *n.* brazen boldness, impudence, insolence. *The customs officials were infuriated by the effrontery of the illegal alien who nonchalantly carried drugs into the country in his shirt pocket.*

effusive (i·'fyoo·siv) *adj.* expressing emotions in an unrestrained or excessive way; profuse, overflowing, gushy. *Anne's unexpected effusive greeting made Tammy uncomfortable.*

egalitarian (i·gal·i·'tair·ee·ăn) *adj.* characterized by or affirming the principle of equal political, social, civil, and economic rights for all persons. *Hannah was moved by the candidate's egalitarian speech.*

egregious (i·'gree·jŭs) *adj.* conspicuously and outrageously bad or offensive; flagrant. *After her egregious accounting error cost the company thousands of dollars, Enid was fired.*

eke (eek) *v.* to get or supplement with great effort or strain; to earn or accomplish laboriously. *Working two jobs enabled Quincy to eke out a living wage for his family.*

élan (ay·'lahn) *n.* 1. vivacity, enthusiasm, vigor. 2. distinctive style or flair. *The new designer's élan and originality were sure to help him succeed in the highly competitive fashion industry.*

elite (i·'leet) *n.* 1. the best or most skilled members of a social group or class. 2. a person or group regarded as superior. *Within the student orchestra, there existed a small group of musical elite who performed around the country.*

eloquent ('el·ŏ·kwĕnt) *adj.* expressing strong emotions or arguments in a powerful, fluent, and persuasive manner. *Abraham Lincoln's Gettysburg Address is considered one of the most eloquent speeches ever given by a U.S. president.*

elusive (i·'loo·siv) *adj.* evasive, eluding the grasp; difficult to capture, describe or comprehend. *The bank robber was not caught during his first crime spree and he proved to be a very elusive fugitive.*

eminent ('em·ĭ·nĕnt) *adj.* towering above or more prominent than others, lofty; standing above others in quality, character, reputation, etc.; distinguished. *The* *chairperson proudly announced that the keynote speaker at the animal rights conven-tion would be the eminent primatologist Jane Goodall.*

empirical (em·'pir·i·kal) *adj.* based on observation or experience rather than the-ory. *Frank's empirical data suggested that mice would climb over the walls of the maze to get to the cheese rather than navigate the maze itself.*

emulate ('em·yŭ·layt) *v.* to try to equal or excel, especially by imitation. *Ricky admired his sister Joan and always tried to emulate her behavior.*

enclave ('en·klayv) *n.* a distinct territory lying wholly within the boundaries of another, larger territory. *The country of Lesotho is an enclave of South Africa.*

endemic (en·'dem·ik) *adj.* 1. prevalent in or characteristic of a specific area or group of people. 2. native to a particular region. *Kudzu, a hairy, purple-flowered vine thought to be endemic to the southeastern United States, was actually imported from Japan.*

enervate ('en·ĕr·vayt) *v.* to weaken, deprive of strength or vitality; to make fee-ble or impotent. *Stephanie's cutting remarks managed to enervate Hasaan.*

engender (en·'jen·dĕr) *v.* to produce, give rise to, bring into existence. *Professor Sorenson's support worked to engender Samantha's desire to pursue a PhD.*

enigma (ĕ·'nig·mă) *n.* something that is puzzling or difficult to understand; a baffling problem or riddle. *The math problem was difficult to solve and proved to be an enigma.*

ennui (ahn·'wee) *n.* boredom and listlessness resulting from something tedious or uninteresting. *The tour guide's façade of enthusiasm could not hide his ennui.*

enormity (i·'nor·mi·tee) *n.* 1. excessive wickedness. 2. a monstrous offense or evil act, atrocity. (Note: *Enormity* is often used to indicate something of great size—e.g., the enormity of the task—but this is considered an incorrect use of the word.) *The enormity of the serial killer's crimes will never be forgotten.*

ensconce (en·'skons) *v.* 1. to fix or settle firmly and securely. 2. to place or hide securely, conceal. *Once the spy was comfortably ensconced in his new identity, he began his secret mission.*

ephemeral (i·'fem·ĕ·răl) *adj.* lasting only a very short time, transitory. *Summer always seems so ephemeral; before you know it, it's time to go back to school again.*

epicurean (ep·i·'kyoor·ee·ăn) *n.* a person devoted to the pursuit of pleasure and luxury, especially the enjoyment of good food and comfort. *While on vacation at a posh resort hotel, Joan became a true epicurean.*

epiphany (i·ˈpif·ă·nee) *n.* 1. a sudden, intuitive realization of the essence or meaning of something, a perceptive revelation. 2. a manifestation of the divine. 3. Epiphany, a Christian feast on the twelfth day after Christmas celebrating the divine manifestation of Jesus to the Magi. *As I listened to Professor Lane's lecture, I had a sudden epiphany that I was in the wrong major.*

epitome (i·ˈpit·ŏ·mee) *n.* 1. something or someone that embodies a particular quality or characteristic, a representative example or a typical model. 2. a brief summary or abstract. *Einstein is the epitome of true genius.*

equanimity (ee·kwă·ˈnim·i·tee) *n.* calmness of temperament, even-temperedness; patience and composure, especially under stressful circumstances. *The hostage negotiator's equanimity during the stand-off was remarkable.*

equivocate (i·ˈkwiv·ŏ·kayt) *v.* to use unclear or ambiguous language in order to mislead or conceal the truth. *Raj tried to equivocate when explaining why he came home after his curfew.*

eradicate (i·ˈrad·ĭ·kayt) *v.* to root out and utterly destroy; to annihilate, exterminate. *The exterminator said he would eradicate the vermin from the house.*

erratic (i·ˈrat·ik) *adj.* 1. moving or behaving in an irregular, uneven, or inconsistent manner. 2. deviating from the normal or typical course of action, opinion, etc. *During an earthquake, a seismograph's needle moves in an erratic manner.*

ersatz (ĕr·ˈzăts) *adj.* artificial; being an imitation or substitute, especially one that is inferior. *Though most of the guests couldn't tell the difference, Waldo knew that the dish was made with ersatz truffles.*

erudite (ˈer·yŭ·dīt) *adj.* having or showing great learning; profoundly educated, scholarly. *The scholarly work of nonfiction was obviously written by an erudite young man.*

ethos (ˈee·thos) *n.* the spirit, attitude, disposition or beliefs characteristic of a community, epoch, region, etc. *The ethos of their group included a commitment to pacifism.*

eulogy (ˈyoo·lŏ·gee) *n.* a formal speech or piece of writing in praise of someone or something. *Richard was asked to give a eulogy for his fallen comrade.*

euphoria (yoo·ˈfohr·ee·ă) *n.* a feeling of well-being or high spirits. *When falling in love, it is not uncommon to experience feelings of euphoria.*

evade (i·ˈvayd) *v.* to elude or avoid by cleverness or deceit. 2. to avoid fulfilling, answering, or doing. *The thief evaded the store's security guards by escaping out the back door.*

evanescent (ev·ă·ˈnes·ĕnt) *adj.* vanishing or tending to vanish like vapor; transitory, fleeting. *The subject of the poem is the evanescent nature of young love.*

evince (i·ˈvins) *v.* to show or demonstrate clearly; to make evident. *The safety officer tried to evince the dangers of driving under the influence by showing pictures of alcohol-related automobile accidents.*

exacerbate (ig·ˈzas·ĕr·bayt) *v.* to make worse; to increase the severity, violence, or bitterness of. *We should have known that splashing salt water on Dan's wound would exacerbate his pain.*

exculpate (eks·ˈkul·payt) *v.* to free from blame, to clear from a charge of guilt. *When Anthony admitted to the crime, it served to exculpate Marcus.*

exigent (ˈek·si·jĕnt) *adj.* 1. urgent, requiring immediate action or attention, critical. 2. requiring much effort or precision, demanding. *The late-night call on Paul's cell phone concerned matters of an exigent nature.*

exorbitant (ig·ˈzor·bi·tănt) *adj.* greatly exceeding the bounds of what is normal or reasonable; inordinate and excessive. *Three thousand dollars is an exorbitant amount to pay for a scarf.*

expedient (ik·ˈspee·dee·ĕnt) *n.* a short-lived means to an end. *adj.* 1. appropriate for a purpose, suitable for a means to an end. 2. serving to promote one's own interests rather than principle. *A quick divorce was an expedient end to the couple's two-month marriage.*

explicit (ik·ˈsplis·it) *adj.* stated clearly and fully; straightforward, exact. *The terms of the rental agreement were explicit in the document.*

expunge (ik·ˈspunj) *v.* to wipe or rub out, delete; to eliminate completely, annihilate. *After finishing probation, juveniles can petition the courts to expunge their criminal records.*

extenuate (ik·ten·ˈyoo·ayt) *v.* to reduce the strength or lessen the seriousness of, to try to partially excuse. *The man's desperation extenuated his actions.*

F

façade (fă·ˈsahd) *n.* 1. the face or front of a building. 2. an artificial or deceptive front, especially one intended to hide something unpleasant. *Antoine's stoicism is just a façade; he is really a deeply emotional person.*

facetious (fă·ˈsee·shŭs) *adj.* humorous and witty, cleverly amusing; jocular, sportive. *Jude's facetious reply angered his teacher but made his classmates laugh.*

fallacy ('fal·ă·see) *n.* 1. a false notion or misconception resulting from incorrect or illogical reasoning. 2. that which is deceptive or has a false appearance; something that misleads, deception. *The "slippery slope" fallacy argues that once X happens, Y and Z will automatically follow.*

fatuous ('fach·oo·ŭs) *adj.* complacently stupid; feeble-minded and silly. *Because Sam was such an intellectually accomplished student, Mr. Britt was surprised to discover that Sam's well-meaning but fatuous parents were not at all like him.*

feckless ('fek·lis) *adj.* 1. lacking purpose or vitality; feeble, weak. 2. incompetent and ineffective, careless. *Jake's feckless performance led to his termination from the team.*

fecund ('fek·ŭnd) *adj.* fertile. *The fecund soil in the valley was able to sustain the growing community.*

feign (fayn) *v.* to pretend, to give the false appearance of. *Walter feigned illness to avoid attending the meeting.*

felicitous (fi·'lis·i·tŭs) *adj.* 1. apt, suitably expressed, apropos. 2. marked by good fortune. *The felicitous turn of events during her promotional tour propelled Susan's book to the best-seller list.*

fervor ('fur·vŏr) *n.* zeal, ardor, intense emotion. *The fervor of the fans in the stands helped propel the team to victory.*

fetter ('fet·ĕr) *v.* 1. to shackle, put in chains. 2. to impede or restrict. *The presence of two security guards fettered their plans to get backstage.*

flaccid ('fla·sid) *adj.* hanging loose or wrinkled; weak, flabby, not firm. *The skin of cadavers becomes flaccid in a matter of hours.*

flippant ('flip·ănt) *adj.* not showing proper seriousness; disrespectful, saucy. *Ursula's flippant remarks in front of her fiancé's parents were an embarrassment to us all.*

florid ('flor·id) *adj.* 1. elaborate, ornate. 2. (of complexion) ruddy, rosy. *The florid architecture in Venice did not appeal to me; I prefer buildings without so much ornamentation.*

flout (flowt) *v.* to disobey openly and scornfully; to reject, mock, go against (as in a tradition or convention). *Flappers in the early twentieth century flouted convention by bobbing their hair and wearing very short skirts.*

forbearance (for·'bair·ăns) *n.* patience, willingness to wait, tolerance. *Gustaf dreaded the security check in the airport, but he faced it with great forbearance because he knew it was for his own safety.*

forestall (fohr·'stawl) *v.* to prevent by taking action first, preempt. *The diplomat was able to forestall a conflict by holding secret meetings with both parties.*

forswear (for·'swair) *v.* 1. to give up, renounce. 2. to deny under oath. *Natasha had to forswear her allegiance to her homeland in order to become a citizen of the new country.*

fortuitous (for·'too·i·tŭs) *adj.* happening by accident or chance; occurring unexpectedly or without any known cause. (Note: *Fortuitous* is commonly used to mean a *happy* accident or an unexpected but *fortunate* occurrence. In its true sense, however, a fortuitous event can be either fortunate or unfortunate.) *By a stroke of fortuitous bad luck, Wei chose a small, exclusive resort for her vacation—only to find that the ex-boyfriend she wanted to get away from had also chosen the same resort.*

frugal ('froo·găl) *adj.* 1. careful and economical, sparing, thrifty. 2. costing little. *My grandparents survived the Great Depression by being very frugal.*

fulminate ('ful·mĭ·nayt) *v.* 1. to issue a thunderous verbal attack, berate. 2. to explode or detonate. *The Senator liked to fulminate when other legislators questioned her ideology.*

fulsome ('fuul·sŏm) *adj.* offensive due to excessiveness, especially excess flattery or praise. *Her new coworker's fulsome attention bothered Kathryn.*

furtive ('fur·tiv) *adj.* 1. characterized by stealth or secrecy, surreptitious. 2. suggesting a hidden motive, shifty. *Harriet's furtive glance told me I had better keep quiet about what I had just seen.*

futile ('fyoo·tĭl) *adj.* useless, producing no result; hopeless, vain. *My mother would never let me attend the party; arguing with her was futile.*

G

gainsay ('gayn·say) *v.* to deny, contradict, or declare false; to oppose. *Petra would gainsay all accusations made against her.*

gargantuan (gahr·'gan·choo·ăn) *adj.* gigantic, huge. *It was a gargantuan supermarket for such a small town.*

garish ('gair·ish) *adj.* excessively bright or over-decorated, gaudy; tastelessly showy. *Though Susan thought Las Vegas was garish, Emily thought it was perfectly beautiful.*

garner ('gahr·nĕr) *v.* to gather and store up; to amass, acquire. *Whitney garnered enough money to buy a used car.*

garrulous ('gar·ŭ·lŭs) *adj.* talkative. *Aunt Midge is as garrulous as they come, so be prepared to listen for hours.*

gauche (gohsh) *adj.* 1. lacking social graces or polish; without tact. 2. clumsy or awkward. *My little brother is so gauche that it's embarrassing to be with him in public.*

genteel (jen·'teel) *adj.* elegantly polite, well bred, refined. *The genteel host made sure that each entrée was cooked to each guest's specifications.*

gerrymander ('jer·i·man·dĕr) *n.* the act of gerrymandering. *v.* to divide an area into voting districts so as to give one party an unfair advantage. *The election was rigged by gerrymandering that gave unfair advantage to the incumbent.*

gestalt (gĕ·shtält) *n.* a configuration or pattern of elements so unified as a whole that it cannot be described merely as a sum of its parts. *One of the fundamental beliefs of gestalt therapy is that we exist in a web of relationships to other things, and that it is possible to understand ourselves only in the context of these relationships.*

gird (gurd) *v.* 1. to encircle or bind with a belt or band. 2. to encompass, surround. 3. to prepare for action, especially military confrontation. 4. to sneer at, mock, gibe. *The negotiations had failed, and the soldiers girded for battle.*

gregarious (grĕ·'gair·ee·ŭs) *adj.* 1. seeking and enjoying the company of others, sociable. 2. tending to form a group with others of the same kind. *Alan used to be so diffident, but now he's as gregarious as can be and is usually the life of the party.*

grovel ('gruv·ĕl) *v.* to lie or creep with one's face to the ground in a servile, humble, or fearful manner. *Panji, if you want your boss to treat you with respect, you've got to stop groveling and stand up for yourself.*

guffaw (gu·'faw) *n.* a noisy, coarse burst of laughter. *Michael let out quite a guffaw when Jamal told him the outlandish joke.*

guile (gīl) *n.* treacherous cunning; shrewd, crafty deceit. *The most infamous pirates displayed tremendous guile.*

H

hallow ('hal·oh) *v.* to make holy, consecrate. *The religious leader hallowed the new worship hall.*

hapless ('hap·lis) *adj.* unlucky, unfortunate. *The hapless circumstances of her journey resulted in lost luggage, missed connections, and a very late arrival.*

harangue (hă·'rang) *n.* a long, often scolding or bombastic speech; a tirade. *v.* to speak in a pompous maner; to declaim. *Members of the audience began to get restless during the senator's political harangue.*

harbinger ('hahr·bin·jĕr) *n.* a person, thing, or event that foreshadows or indicates what is to come; a forerunner or precursor. *The arrival of the robins is a harbinger of spring.*

harrowing ('har·oh·ing) *adj.* distressing, creating great stress or torment. *The turbulent flight proved to be a harrowing experience for Jane.*

haughty ('haw·tee) *adj.* scornfully arrogant and condescending; acting as though one is superior and others unworthy, disdainful. *Stanley is so often haughty that he has very few friends.*

hegemony (hi·'jem·ŏ·nee) *n.* predominant influence or leadership, especially of one government over others. *The hegemony of his country borders on imperialism.*

hermetic (hur·'met·ik) *adj.* 1. having an airtight closure. 2. protected from outside influences. *In the hermetic world of the remote mountain village, the inhabitants did not even know that their country was on the brink of war.*

hiatus (hī·'ay·tŭs) *n.* a gap or opening; an interruption or break. *After he was laid off by the bank, Kobitu decided to take a long hiatus from the financial world and took a job as a middle school math teacher.*

hone (hohn) *v.* to sharpen; to perfect, make more effective. *By practicing creating spreadsheets, I honed my computer skills.*

hubris ('hyoo·bris) *n.* overbearing pride or presumption. *In the Greek tragedy* Oedipus Rex, *Oedipus's hubris leads to his downfall.*

I

iconoclast (ī·'kon·oh·klast) *n.* 1. a person who attacks and seeks to overthrow traditional ideas, beliefs, or institutions. 2. someone who opposes and destroys idols used in worship. *Using words as weapons, the well-spoken iconoclast challenged political hypocrisy and fanaticism wherever she found it.*

ignoble (ig·'noh·bĕl) *adj.* 1. lacking nobility in character or purpose, dishonorable. 2. not of the nobility, common. *Mark was an ignoble successor to such a well-respected leader, and many members of the organization resigned.*

ignominious (ig·nŏ·'min·ee·ŭs) *adj.* 1. marked by shame or disgrace. 2. deserving disgrace or shame; despicable. *The evidence of plagiarism brought an ignominious end to what had been a notable career for the talented young author.*

imbroglio (im·'brohl·yoh) *n.* a confused or difficult situation, usually involving a disagreement or misunderstanding. *In Shakespeare's comedies, there is often an imbroglio caused by a case of mistaken identity.*

immolate ('im·ŏ·layt) *v.* 1. to kill, as a sacrifice. 2. to kill (oneself) by fire. 3. to destroy (one thing for another). *In order for the plants to grow, I had to immolate the weeds.*

impasse ('im·pas) *n.* a deadlock, stalemate; a difficulty without a solution. *The labor negotiations with management reached an impasse, and a strike seemed imminent.*

impassive (im·'pas·iv) *adj.* not showing or feeling emotion or pain. *It was hard to know what she was feeling by looking at the impassive expression on her face.*

impecunious (im·pĕ·'kyoo·nee·ŭs) *adj.* having little or no money; poor, penniless. *Many impecunious immigrants to the United States eventually are able to make comfortable lives for themselves.*

imperialism (im·'peer·ee·ă·liz·ĕm) *n.* the policy of extending the rule or authority of a nation or empire by acquiring other territories or dependencies. *Great Britain embraced imperialism, acquiring so many territories that the sun never set on the British Empire.*

imperious (im·'peer·ee·ŭs) *adj.* overbearing, bossy, domineering. *Stella was relieved with her new job transfer because she would no longer be under the control of such an imperious boss.*

impervious (im·'pur·vee·ŭs) *adj.* 1. incapable of being penetrated. 2. not able to be influenced or affected. *Hadley is such a diehard libertarian that he is impervious to any attempts to change his beliefs.*

impetuous (im·'pech·oo·ŭs) *adj.* 1. characterized by sudden, forceful energy or emotion; impulsive, unduly hasty and without thought. 2. marked by violent force. *It was an impetuous decision to run off to Las Vegas and get married after a one-week courtship.*

implacable (im·'plak·ă·bĕl) *adj.* incapable of being placated or appeased; inexorable. *Some of the people who call the customer service desk for assistance are implacable, but most are relatively easy to serve.*

importune (im·por·'toon) *v.* 1. to ask incessantly, make incessant requests. 2. to beg persistently and urgently. *Children can't help but importune during the holidays, constantly nagging for the irresistible toys they see advertised on television.*

imprecation (im·prĕ·'kay·shŏn) *n.* an invocation of evil, a curse. *In the book I'm reading, the gypsy queen levies an imprecation on the lead character.*

impudent ('im·pyŭ·dĕnt) *adj.* 1. boldly showing a lack of respect, insolent. 2. shamelessly forward, immodest. *Thumbing his nose at the principal was an impudent act.*

impugn (im·'pyoon) *v.* to attack as false or questionable; to contradict or call into question. *The editorial impugned the senator's reelection platform and set the tone for the upcoming debate.*

impute (im·'pyoot) *v.* to attribute to a cause or source, ascribe, credit. *Doctors impute the reduction in cancer deaths to the nationwide decrease in cigarette smoking.*

incense ('in·sens) *n.* fragrant material that gives off scents when burned. (in·'sens) *v.* to make (someone) angry. *Marcel's criticism incensed his coworker.*

incendiary (in·'sen·dee·er·ee) *adj.* 1. causing or capable of causing fire; burning readily. 2. of or involving arson. 3. tending to incite or inflame, inflammatory. *Fire marshals checked for incendiary devices in the theater after they received an anonymous warning.*

inchoate (in·'koh·it) *adj.* 1. just begun; in an initial or early stage of development, incipient. 2. not yet fully formed, undeveloped, incomplete. *During the inchoate stage of fetal growth, it is difficult to distinguish between a cow, a frog, or a human; as they mature, the developing embryos take on the characteristics of their own particular species.*

incognito (in·kog·née·toh) *adj.* or *adv.* with one's identity concealed; in disguise or under an assumed character or identity. *The star was traveling incognito, hoping to find some measure of privacy on her vacation.*

incontrovertible (in·kon·trŏ·'vur·tĭ·bĕl) *adj.* indisputable, undeniable. *The photographs showed Brad and Allison together; their relationship was an incontrovertible fact.*

incredulous (in·'krej·ŭ·lŭs) *adj.* skeptical, unwilling to believe. *The members of the jury were incredulous when they heard the defendant's farfetched explanation of the crime.*

inculcate (in·'kul·kayt) *v.* to teach and impress by frequent instruction or repetition; to indoctrinate, instill. *My parents worked hard to inculcate in me a deep sense of responsibility to others.*

incursion (in·'kur·zhŏn) *n.* a raid or temporary invasion of someone else's territory; the act of entering or running into a territory or domain. *There was an incursion on the western border of their country.*

indefatigable (in·di·ˈfat·ĭ·gă·bĕl) *adj.* not easily exhausted or fatigued; tireless. *The volunteers were indefatigable; they worked until every piece of trash was removed from the beach.*

indolent (ˈin·dŏ·lĕnt) *adj.* 1. lazy, lethargic, inclined to avoid labor. 2. causing little or no pain; slow to grow or heal. *The construction foreman was hesitant to hire Earl because of his reputation of being indolent.*

indomitable (in·ˈdom·i·tă·bĕl) *adj.* not able to be vanquished or overcome, unconquerable; not easily discouraged or subdued. *The indomitable spirit of the Olympic athletes was inspirational.*

ineluctable (in·i·ˈluk·tă·bĕl) *adj.* certain, inevitable; not to be avoided or overcome. *The ineluctable outcome of the two-person race was that there would be one winner and one loser.*

inept (in·ˈept) *adj.* 1. not suitable, inappropriate. 2. absurd, foolish. 3. incompetent, bungling and clumsy. *Trying to carry all her suitcases at once was an inept way for Amanda to save time.*

infidel (ˈin·fi·dĕl) *n.* 1. a person with no religious beliefs. 2. a nonbeliever, one who does not accept a particular religion, doctrine, or system of beliefs. *Because he did not subscribe to the beliefs of the party, the members considered him an infidel.*

ingenuous (in·ˈjen·yoo·ŭs) *adj.* 1. not cunning or deceitful, unable to mask feelings; artless, frank, sincere. 2. lacking sophistication or worldliness. *Don's expression of regret was ingenuous, for even though he didn't know her well, he felt a deep sadness when Mary died.*

inimitable (i·ˈnim·i·tă·bĕl) *adj.* defying imitation, unmatchable. *His performance on the tennis court was inimitable, and he won three championships.*

inscrutable (in·ˈscroo·tă·bĕl) *adj.* baffling, unfathomable, incapable of being understood. *It was completely inscrutable how the escape artist got out of the trunk.*

insolent (ˈin·sŏ·lĕnt) *adj.* haughty and contemptuous; brazen, disrespectful, impertinent. *Parents of teenagers often observe the insolent behavior that typically accompanies adolescence.*

insouciant (in·ˈsoo·see·ănt) *adj.* blithely unconcerned or carefree; nonchalant, indifferent. *Julian's insouciant attitude about his finances will get him in trouble someday.*

interdict (in·tĕr·ˈdikt) *v.* to prohibit, forbid. *Carlos argued that the agriculture department should interdict plans to produce genetically modified foods.*

intractable (in·'trak·tă·bĕl) *adj.* unmanageable, unruly, stubborn. *The young colt was intractable, and training had to be cancelled temporarily.*

intransigent (in·'tran·si·jĕnt) *adj.* unwilling to compromise, stubborn. *Young children can be intransigent when it comes to what foods they will eat, insisting on familiar favorites and rejecting anything new.*

intrepid (in·'trep·id) *adj.* fearless, brave, undaunted. *Hunger had made the caveman intrepid, and he faced the mammoth without fear.*

inured (in·'yoord) *adj.* accustomed to, adapted. *Trisha had become inured to her boss's criticism, and it no longer bothered her.*

inveigle (in·'vay·gĕl) *v.* to influence or persuade through gentle coaxing or flattery; to entice. *Vanessa inveigled her way into a promotion that should have gone to Maxon.*

inveterate (in·'vet·ĕ·rit) *adj.* habitual; deep rooted, firmly established. *I am an inveterate pacifist and am unlikely to change my mind.*

involute ('in·vŏ·loot) *adj.* intricate, complex. *The tax reform committee faces an extremely involute problem if it wants to distribute the tax burden equally.*

iota (ī·'oh·tă) *n.* a very small amount; the smallest possible quantity. *Professor Carlton is so unpopular because he doesn't have one iota of respect for his students.*

irascible (i·'ras·ĭ·bĕl) *adj.* irritable, easily aroused to anger, hot tempered. *Her irascible temperament caused many problems with the staff at the office.*

ire (īr) *n.* anger, wrath. *I was filled with ire when Vladimir tried to take credit for my work.*

irk (urk) *v.* to annoy, irritate, vex. *Being a teenager means being continually irked by your parents—and vice versa.*

irresolute (i·'rez·ŏ·loot) *adj.* feeling or showing uncertainty; hesitant, indecisive. *Sandra is still irresolute, so if you talk to her, you might help her make up her mind.*

J

jargon ('jahr·gŏn) *n.* 1. specialized or technical language of a specific trade or group. 2. nonsensical or meaningless talk. *The technical manual was full of a lot of computer jargon.*

jejune (ji·'joon) *adj.* lacking substance, meager; hence: (a) lacking in interest or significance; insipid or dull (b) lacking in maturity, childish (c) lacking nutritional value. *The movie's trite and overly contrived plot make it a jejune sequel to what was a powerful and novel film.*

jocund ('jok·ŭnd) *adj.* merry, cheerful; sprightly and lighthearted. *Alexi's jocund nature makes it a pleasure to be near her.*

juggernaut ('jug·ĕr·nawt) *n.* 1. a massive, overwhelmingly powerful and unstoppable force that seems to crush everything in its path. 2. Juggernaut, title for the Hindu god Krishna. *A shroud of fear covered Eastern Europe as the juggernaut of communism spread from nation to nation.*

L

laconic (lă·'kon·ik) *adj.* brief and to the point; succinct, terse, concise, often to the point of being curt or brusque. *Zse's laconic reply made it clear that he did not want to discuss the matter any further.*

laissez-faire (les·ay 'fair) *adj.* hands-off; noninterference by the government in business and economic affairs. *Raheeb's laissez-faire management style is not only popular with our employees but also very successful—employee satisfaction is high and profits are up for the third quarter in a row.*

languish ('lang·gwish) *v.* 1. to lose vigor or strength; to become languid, feeble, weak. 2. to exist or continue in a miserable or neglected state. *Lucinda languished in despair when Sven told her he'd fallen in love with another woman.*

latent ('lay·tĕnt) *adj.* present or in existence but not active or evident. *Julian's latent musical talent surfaced when his parents bought an old piano at a garage sale and he started playing.*

lax (laks) *adj.* 1. lacking in rigor or strictness; lenient. 2. not taut or rigid; flaccid, slack. *If parents are too lax with their toddlers, chances are they will have a lot of trouble once they enter school, where the children must follow a long list of rules and regulations.*

liaison (lee·'ay·zon, 'lee·ă·zon) *n.* 1. a channel or means of connection or communication between two groups; one who maintains such communication. 2. a close relationship or link, especially one that is secretive or adulterous. *I have been elected to be the liaison between the union members and management.*

libertine ('lib·ĕr·teen) *n.* one who lives or acts in an immoral or irresponsible way; one who acts according to his or her own impulses and desires and is unrestrained by conventions or morals. *They claim to be avant-garde, but in my opinion, they're just a bunch of libertines.*

lilliputian (lil·i·'pyoo·shăn) *adj.* 1. very small, tiny. 2. trivial or petty. *My troubles are lilliputian compared to hers, and I am thankful that I do not have such major issues in my life.*

loquacious (loh·'kway·shŭs) *adj.* talkative, garrulous. *The loquacious woman sitting next to me on the six-hour flight talked the entire time.*

lucid ('loo·sid) *adj.* 1. very clear, easy to understand, intelligible. 2. sane or rational. *Andrea presented a very lucid argument that proved her point beyond a shadow of a doubt.*

lucrative ('loo·kră·tiv) *adj.* profitable, producing much money. *Teaching is a very rewarding career, but unfortunately it is not very lucrative.*

lugubrious (luu·'goo·bree·ŭs) *adj.* excessively dismal or mournful, often exaggeratedly or ridiculously so. *Irina's lugubrious tears made me believe that her sadness was just a façade.*

M

machination (mak·ĭ·'nay·shŏn) *n.* 1. the act of plotting or devising. 2. a crafty or cunning scheme devised to achieve a sinister end. *Macbeth's machinations failed to bring him the glory he coveted and brought him only tragedy instead.*

maim (maym) *v.* to wound, cripple, or injure, especially by depriving of the use of a limb or other part of the body; to mutilate, disfigure, disable. *The mining accident severely maimed Antol.*

maladroit (mal·ă·'droit) *adj.* clumsy, bungling, inept. *The maladroit waiter broke a dozen plates and spilled coffee on two customers.*

malaise (mă·'layz) *n.* a feeling of illness or unease. *After several tests, Wella finally learned the cause of her malaise: She was allergic to her new Siamese cat.*

malapropism ('mal·ă·prop·iz·ĕm) *n.* comical misuse of words, especially those that are similar in sound. *His malapropisms may make us laugh, but they won't win our vote.*

malfeasance (măl·'fee·zăns) *n.* misconduct or wrongdoing, especially by a public official; improper professional conduct. *The city comptroller was found guilty of malfeasance and was removed from office.*

malinger (mă·'ling·gĕr) *v.* to pretend to be injured or ill in order to avoid work. *Stop malingering and give me a hand with this job.*

malleable ('mal·ee·ă·bĕl) *adj.* 1. easily molded or pressed into shape. 2. easily controlled or influenced. 3. easily adapting to changing circumstances. *You should be able to convince Xiu quickly; she's quite a malleable person.*

mar (mahr) *v.* 1. to impair or damage, make defective or imperfect. 2. to spoil the perfection or integrity of. *The strident sounds of Omar's abysmal saxophone playing marred the serenity of the afternoon.*

maverick ('mav·ĕr·ik) *n.* rebel, nonconformist, one who acts independently. *Madonna has always been a maverick in the music industry.*

meander (mee·'an·dĕr) *v.* 1. to move on a winding or turning course. 2. to wander about, move aimlessly or without a fixed direction or course. *I meandered through the park for hours, trying to figure out how I could have made such an egregious mistake.*

mélange (may·'lahnzh) *n.* a mixture or assortment. *The eclectic mélange of people at the party made for a scintillating evening.*

mellifluous (me·'lif·loo·ŭs) *adj.* sounding sweet and flowing; honeyed. *Her mellifluous voice floated in through the windows and made everyone smile.*

mendacity (men·'das·i·tee) *n.* 1. the tendency to be dishonest or untruthful. 2. a falsehood or lie. *Carlos's mendacity has made him very unpopular with his classmates, who don't feel they can trust him.*

mercurial (mĕr·'kyoor·ee·ăl) *adj.* 1. liable to change moods suddenly. 2. lively, changeable, volatile. *Fiona is so mercurial that you never know what kind of reaction to expect.*

meretricious (mer·ĕ·'trish·ŭs) *adj.* gaudy, tawdry; showily attractive but false or insincere. *With its casinos and attractions, some people consider Las Vegas the most meretricious city in the country.*

mete (meet) *v.* to distribute, allot, apportion. *The punishments were meted out fairly to everyone involved in the plot.*

meticulous (mĕ·'tik·yŭ·lŭs) *adj.* extremely careful and precise; paying great attention to detail. *Tibor was awed by the meticulous detail in the painting—it looked as real as a photograph.*

mettlesome ('met·ĕl·sŏm) *adj.* courageous, high-spirited. *Alice's mettlesome attitude was infectious and inspired us all to press on.*

milieu (meel·'yuu) *n.* environment or setting. *The milieu at the writer's retreat is designed to inspire creativity.*

mince (mins) *v.* 1. to cut into very small pieces. 2. to walk or speak affectedly, as with studied refinement. 3. to say something more delicately or indirectly for the sake of politeness or decorum. *Please don't mince your words—just tell me what you want to say.*

minutiae (mĭ·nōō'shē·a) *n., pl.* very small details; trivial or trifling matters. *His attention to the minutiae of the process enabled him to make his great discovery.*

mirth (murth) *n.* great merriment, joyous laughter. *The joyous wedding celebration filled the reception hall with mirth throughout the evening.*

misanthrope ('mis·an·throhp) *n.* one who hates or distrusts humankind. *Pay no mind to his criticism; he's a real misanthrope, and no one can do anything right in his eyes.*

miscreant ('mis·kree·ănt) *n.* a villain, criminal; evil person. *The miscreant had eluded the police for months, but today he was finally captured.*

mitigate ('mit·ĭ·gayt) *v.* 1. to make less intense or severe. 2. to moderate the force or intensity of, soften, diminish, alleviate. *I am sure that if you tell the headmaster the truth, the extenuating circumstances will mitigate the severity of your punishment.*

mollify ('mol·ĭ·fī) *v.* 1. to soothe the anger of, calm. 2. to lessen in intensity. 3. to soften, make less rigid. *The crying child was quickly mollified by her mother.*

moot (moot) *adj.* debatable, undecided. *Although this is a moot issue, it is one that is often debated among certain circles.*

morose (mŏ·'rohs) *adj.* gloomy, sullen, melancholy. *My daughter has been morose ever since our dog ran away.*

multifarious (mul·ti·'fair·ee·ŭs) *adj.* very varied, greatly diversified; having many aspects. *The job requires the ability to handle multifarious tasks.*

mundane (mun·'dayn) *adj.* 1. ordinary, commonplace, dull. 2. worldly, secular, not spiritual. *If you do not have passion for your job, going to work each day can become mundane.*

myriad ('mir·ee·ăd) *adj.* too numerous to be counted; innumerable. *n.* an indefinitely large number; an immense number, vast amount. *To the refugees from Somalia, the myriad choices in the American supermarket were overwhelming.*

N

nadir ('nay·dĭr) *n.* the very bottom, the lowest point. *When he felt he was at the nadir of his life, Robert began to practice mediation to elevate his spirits.*

narcissism ('narh·si·siz·ĕm) *n.* admiration or worship of oneself; excessive interest in one's own personal features. *Some critics say that movie stars are guilty of narcissism.*

nascent ('nas·ĕnt) *adj.* coming into existence, emerging. *The nascent movement gathered strength quickly and soon became a nationwide call to action.*

nemesis ('nem·ĕ·sis) *n.* 1. source of harm or ruin, the cause of one's misery or downfall; bane. 2. agent of retribution or vengeance. *In* Frankenstein, *the monster Victor creates becomes his nemesis.*

nexus ('nek·sŭs) *n.* 1. a means of connection, a link or tie between a series of things. 2. a connected series or group. 3. the core or center. *The nexus between the lobbyists and the recent policy changes is clear.*

noisome ('noi·sŏm) *adj.* 1. offensive, foul, especially in odor; putrid. 2. harmful, noxious. *What a noisome odor is coming from that garbage can!*

non sequitur (non 'sek·wi·tŭr) *n.* a conclusion that does not logically follow from the evidence. *Marcus's argument started off strong, but it degenerated into a series of non sequiturs.*

nonchalant (non·shă·'lahnt) *adj.* indifferent or cool, not showing anxiety or excitement. *Victoria tried to be nonchalant, but I could tell she was nervous.*

novel ('nov·ĕl) *n.* a genre of literature. *adj.* strikingly new, original, or different. *The chef's new idea to add mango to the salad was novel.*

noxious ('nok·shŭs) *adj.* unpleasant and harmful, unwholesome. *The noxious smell drove everyone from the room.*

nullify ('nul·ĭ·fī) *v.* 1. to make null (without legal force), invalidate. 2. to counteract or neutralize the effect of. *The opponents wanted to nullify the bill before it became a law.*

O

obdurate ('ob·dŭ·rit) *adj.* stubborn and inflexible; hardhearted, not easily moved to pity. *I doubt he'll change his mind; he's the most obdurate person I know.*

obfuscate (ob·'fus·kayt) *v.* 1. to make obscure or unclear, to muddle or make difficult to understand. 2. to dim or darken. *Instead of clarifying the matter, Walter only obfuscated it further.*

obsequious (ŏb·'see·kwee·ŭs) *adj.* excessively or ingratiatingly compliant or submissive; attentive in a servile or ingratiating manner, fawning. *The obsequious manner of the butler made it clear that he resented his position.*

obstreperous (ob·'strep·ĕ·rŭs) *adj.* noisily and stubbornly defiant; aggressively boisterous, unruly. *The obstreperous child refused to go to bed.*

obtrusive (ŏb·'troo·siv) *adj.* 1. prominent, undesirably noticeable. 2. projecting, thrusting out. 3. tending to push one's self or one's ideas upon others, forward, intrusive. *Thankfully, Minsun survived the accident, but she was left with several obtrusive scars.*

obtuse (ŏb·'toos) *adj.* 1. stupid and slow to understand. 2. blunt, not sharp or pointed. *Please don't be so obtuse; you know what I mean.*

obviate ('ob·vee·ayt) *v.* to make unnecessary, get rid of. *Hiring Magdalena would obviate the need to hire a music tutor, for she is also a classical pianist.*

occult (ŏ·'kult) *adj.* 1. secret, hidden, concealed. 2. involving the realm of the supernatural. 3. beyond ordinary understanding, incomprehensible. *The embezzler was good at keeping his financial records occult from the authorities.*

odious ('oh·di·ŭs) *adj.* contemptible, hateful, detestable. *Zachary found the work in the slaughterhouse so odious that he quit after one day and became a vegetarian.*

oeuvre ('uu·vrĕ) *n.* 1. a work of art. 2. the total lifework of a writer, artist, composer, etc. *Constanta's latest oeuvre is an avant-garde symphony featuring a cow bell solo.*

officious (ŏ·'fish·ŭs) *adj.* meddlesome, bossy; eagerly offering unnecessary or unwanted advice. *My officious Aunt Midge is coming to the party, so be prepared for lots of questions and advice.*

oligarchy ('ol·ĭ·gahr·kee) *n.* form of government in which the power is in the hands of a select few. *The small governing body calls itself a democracy, but it is clearly an oligarchy.*

omnipotent (om·'nip·ŏ·tĕnt) *adj.* having unlimited or universal power or force. *In Greek mythology, Zeus was the most powerful god, but he was not omnipotent, because even his rule was often held in check by the unchangeable laws of the Three Fates.*

omniscient (om·'nish·ĕnt) *adj.* having infinite knowledge; knowing all things. *In a story with an omniscient narrator, we can hear the thoughts and feelings of all of the characters.*

onus ('oh·nŭs) *n.* duty or responsibility of doing something; task, burden. *It was Clark's idea, so the onus is on him to show us that it will work.*

opprobrious (ŏ·'proh·bree·ŭs) *adj.* 1. expressing contempt or reproach; scornful, abusive. 2. bringing shame or disgrace. *It was inappropriate to make such opprobrious remarks in front of everybody.*

opulent ('op·yŭ·lĕnt) *adj.* 1. possessing great wealth, affluent. 2. abundant, luxurious. *Lee is very wealthy, but he does not live an opulent lifestyle.*

oscillate ('os·ĭ·layt) *v.* 1. to swing back and forth or side to side in a steady, uninterrupted rhythm. 2. to waver, as between two conflicting options or opinions; vacillate. *The rhythm of the oscillating fan put the baby to sleep.*

ostensible (o·'sten·sĭ·bĕl) *adj.* seeming, appearing as such, put forward (as of a reason) but not necessarily so; pretended. *The ostensible reason for the meeting is to discuss the candidates, but I believe they have already made their decision.*

ostracize ('os·tră·sīz) *v.* to reject, cast out from a group or from society. *Kendall was ostracized after he repeatedly stole from his friends.*

overweening (oh·vĕr·'wee·ning) *adj.* 1. presumptuously arrogant, overbearing. 2. excessive, immoderate. *I quit because I couldn't stand to work for such an overweening boss.*

oxymoron (oks·ee·'moh·rŏn) *n.* a figure of speech containing a seemingly contradictory combination of expressions, such as *friendly fire*. *The term* nonworking mother *is a contemptible oxymoron.*

P

palliate ('pal·ee·ayt) *v.* 1. to make something less intense or severe, mitigate, alleviate; to gloss over, put a positive spin on. 2. to provide relief from pain, relieve the symptoms of a disease or disorder. *The governor tried to palliate his malfeasance, but it soon became clear that he would not be able to prevent a scandal.*

pallor ('pal·ŏr) *n.* paleness, lack of color. *The fever subsided, but her pallor remained for several weeks.*

paltry ('pawl·tree) *adj.* 1. lacking in importance or worth, insignificant; contemptibly small in amount. 2. wretched or contemptible, pitiful. *Walton couldn't believe the billionaire offered such a paltry reward for the return of his lost dog.*

paradigm ('par·ă·dīm) *n.* 1. something that serves as a model or example. 2. set of assumptions, beliefs, values or practices that constitutes a way of understanding or doing things. *Elected "Employee of the Month," Winona is a paradigm of efficiency.*

par excellence (pahr 'ek·sĕ·lahns) *adj.* being the best or truest of its kind, quintessential; having the highest degree of excellence, beyond comparison. *Bob Hope was an entertainer par excellence.*

pariah (pă·'rī·ă) *n.* an outcast, a rejected and despised person. *After he told a sexist joke, Jason was treated like a pariah by all of the women in the office.*

partisan ('pahr·ti·zăn) *n.* 1. a person fervently and often uncritically supporting a group or cause. 2. a guerilla, a member of an organized body of fighters who attack or harass an enemy. *The partisan lobby could not see the logic of the opposing senator's argument and did not understand how the proposed legislation would infringe upon basic constitutional rights.*

paucity ('paw·si·tee) *n.* scarcity, smallness of supply or quantity. *The paucity of food in the area drove the herd farther and farther to the south.*

parvenu ('pahr·vĕ·noo) *n.* a person who has suddenly risen to a higher social or economic status but has not been socially accepted by others in that class; an upstart. *Ronnel was nice enough, of course, but because he was "new money" in an "old money" town, he was a parvenu who struggled to be accepted by his wealthy peers.*

peccadillo (pek·ă·'dil·oh) *n.* a trivial offense, a small sin or fault. *Don't make such a big deal out of a little peccadillo.*

pecuniary (pi·'kyoo·nee·er·ee) *adj.* of, relating to, or involving money. *Rosen was relieved to learn that his penalty would be pecuniary only and that he would not have to spend any time in jail.*

pedantic (pi·'dăn·tik) *n.* a walker *adj.* marked by a narrow, tiresome focus on or display of learning, especially of rules or trivial matters. *Her lessons were so pedantic that I found I was easily bored.*

pedestrian (pĕ·'des·tri·ăn) *n.* a walker. *adj.* commonplace, trite; unremarkable, unimaginative, dull. *Although the film received critical acclaim, its pedestrian plot has been overused by screenwriters for decades.*

pellucid (pĕ·'loo·sid) *adj.* 1. translucent, able to be seen through with clarity. 2. (e.g., of writing) very clear, easy to understand. *Senator Waterson's pellucid argument made me change my vote.*

penchant ('pen·chănt) *n.* a strong liking or inclination (for something). *Consuela has a penchant for wearing the latest fashions.*

pensive ('pen·siv) *adj.* deeply thoughtful, especially in a serious or melancholy manner. *After the terrible car accident, Anoki was pensive about what he should do with his life.*

penultimate (pi·'nul·tĭ·mit) *adj.* next to last. *There's a real surprise for the audience in the penultimate scene.*

penury ('pen·yŭ·ree) *n.* extreme poverty, destitution. *After ten years of penury, it's good to be financially secure again.*

peremptory (pĕ·'remp·tŏ·ree) *adj.* 1. offensively self-assured, dictatorial. 2. commanding, imperative, not allowing contradiction or refusal. 3. putting an end to debate or action. *The mother's peremptory tone ended the children's bickering.*

perfidious (pĕr·'fid·ee·ŭs) *adj.* treacherous, dishonest; violating good faith, disloyal. *The perfidious knight betrayed his king.*

perfunctory (pĕr·'fungk·tŏ·ree) *adj.* done out of a sense of duty or routine but without much care or interest; superficial, not thorough. *We were not satisfied with his perfunctory work; we felt a more thorough job could have been done.*

perjury ('pur·jŭ·ree) *n.* the deliberate willful giving of false, misleading, or incomplete testimony while under oath. *William was convicted of perjury for lying about his whereabouts on the night of the crime.*

pernicious (pĕr·'nish·ŭs) *adj.* deadly, harmful, very destructive. *Nancy's opponent started a pernicious rumor that destroyed her chances of winning.*

personable ('pur·sŏ·nă·bĕl) *adj.* pleasing in appearance or manner, attractive. *Sandra is personable and well liked by her peers.*

pertinacious (pur·tĭ·'nay·shŭs) *adj.* extremely stubborn or persistent; holding firmly to a belief, purpose, or course of action. *The pertinacious journalist finally uncovered the truth about the factory's illegal disposal of toxins.*

pervade (pĕr·'vayd) *v.* to spread everywhere, permeate; to be diffused or present throughout. *Fear pervaded the classroom after Sally started a rumor that Mr. Higgins would be their new teacher.*

petrify ('pet·rĭ·fī) *v.* 1. to make hard or stiff like a stone. 2. to stun or paralyze with fear, astonishment, or dread. *I was petrified when I heard the door open in the middle of the night.*

petulant ('pech·ŭ·lănt) *adj.* peevish; unreasonably or easily irritated or annoyed. *The pouting and sulking child could only be described as petulant.*

philistine ('fil·i·steen) *n.* a smug, ignorant person; someone who is uncultured and commonplace. *Richards thinks he is cosmopolitan, but he's really just a philistine.*

phoenix ('fee·niks) *n.* 1. a person or thing of unmatched beauty or excellence. 2. a person or thing that has become renewed or restored after suffering calamity or apparent annihilation (after the mythological bird that periodically immolated itself and rose from the ashes as a new phoenix). *The phoenix is often used to symbolize something that is indomitable or immortal.*

pillage ('pil·ij) *v.* to forcibly rob of goods, especially in time of war; to plunder. *The barbarians pillaged the village before destroying it with fire.*

piquant ('pee·kănt) *adj.* 1. agreeably pungent, sharp or tart in taste. 2. pleasantly stimulating or provocative. *The spicy shrimp salad is wonderfully piquant.*

pique (peek) *v.* 1. to wound (someone's) pride, to offend. 2. to arouse or provoke. *The article really piqued my interest in wildlife preservation.*

pith (pith) *n.* 1. the essential or central part; the heart or essence (of the matter, idea, experience, etc.). 2. (in biology) the soft, spongelike central cylinder of the stems of most flowering plants. *Her brief, but concise, statement went right to the pith of the argument and covered the most important issues.*

pivotal ('piv·ŏ·tăl) *adj.* being of vital importance, crucial. *We are at a pivotal point in the negotiations and must proceed very carefully; the wrong move now could ruin everything.*

placid ('plas·id) *adj.* calm and peaceful; free from disturbance or tumult. *Lake Placid is as calm and peaceful as its name suggests.*

plaintive ('playn·tiv) *adj.* expressing sorrow; mournful, melancholy. *Janice's plaintive voice made me decide to stay and comfort her longer.*

platitude ('plat·i·tood) *n.* a trite or banal statement, especially one uttered as if it were new. *Matthew offered me several platitudes but no real advice.*

plethora ('pleth·ŏ·ră) *n.* an overabundance, extreme excess. *There was a plethora of food at the reception.*

poignant ('poin·yănt) *adj.* 1. arousing emotion, deeply moving, touching. 2. keenly distressing; piercing or incisive. *They captured the poignant reunion on film.*

polemical (pŏ·'lem·ik·ăl) *adj.* controversial, argumentative. *The analyst presented a highly polemical view of the economic situation.*

poseur (poh·'zur) *n*. someone who takes on airs to impress others; a phony. *My first impression of the arrogant newcomer told me that he was a poseur; I just had a hunch that he wasn't what he seemed to be.*

pragmatic (prag·'mat·ik) *adj*. practical, matter-of-fact; favoring utility. *Because we don't have money or time to waste, I think we should take the most pragmatic approach.*

precarious (pri·'kair·ee·ŭs) *adj*. 1. fraught with danger. 2. dangerously unsteady or insecure. *The crocodile hunter is constantly placing himself in very precarious positions.*

precept ('pree·sept) *n*. a rule establishing standards of conduct. *The headmaster reviewed the precepts of the school with the students.*

precipitous (pri·'sip·i·tŭs) *adj*. 1. extremely steep, dropping sharply. 2. hasty, rash, foolhardy. *Driving through the state park, we spotted a grizzly bear on a precipitous cliff and wondered if he would fall.*

pretentious (pri·'ten·shŭs) *adj*. showy, pompous, putting on airs. *Hannah thinks that being pretentious will make people like her, but she is sorely mistaken.*

prevaricate (pri·'var·i·kayt) *v*. to tell lies, to stray from or evade the truth. *Quit prevaricating and tell me what really happened.*

primeval (prī·'mee·văl) *adj*. ancient, original, belonging to the earliest ages. *The primeval art found in the caves was discovered by accident.*

pristine ('pris·teen) *adj*. 1. in its original and unspoiled condition, unadulterated. 2. clean, pure, free from contamination. *We were awed by the beauty of the pristine forest in northern Canada.*

prodigal ('prod·i·găl) *adj*. 1. recklessly wasteful or extravagant, especially with money. 2. given in great abundance, lavish or profuse. *His prodigal actions led to his financial ruin.*

profligate ('prof·li·git) *adj*. 1. recklessly wasteful or extravagant, prodigal. 2. lacking moral restraint, dissolute. *The profligate man quickly depleted his fortune.*

proletariat (proh·lĕ·'tair·ee·ăt) *n*. the working class, those who do manual labor to earn a living. *The proletariats demanded fewer hours and better wages.*

propinquity (proh·'ping·kwi·tee) *n*. 1. proximity, nearness. 2. affinity, similarity in nature. *The propinquity of these two elements make them difficult to tell apart.*

propitious (proh·'pish·ŭs) *adj*. auspicious, presenting favorable circumstances. *These are propitious omens and foretell a good journey.*

prosaic (proh·'zay·ik) *adj.* unimaginative, ordinary, dull. *The prosaic novel was rejected by the publisher.*

proscribe (proh·'skrīb) *v.* 1. to prohibit, forbid; to banish or outlaw. 2. to denounce or condemn. *The king proscribed the worship of idols in his kingdom.*

proselytize ('pros·ĕ·li·tīz) *v.* to convert or seek to convert someone to another religion, belief, doctrine or cause. *After a few minutes, it became clear to Hannah that the purpose of the meeting was really to proselytize as many attendees as possible.*

protean ('proh·tee·ăn) *adj.* taking many forms, changeable; variable, versatile. *In Native American mythology, the coyote is often called the "shape shifter" because he is such a protean character.*

protocol ('proh·tŏ·kawl) *n.* 1. etiquette, ceremony, or procedure with regard to people's rank or status. 2. a first copy of a treaty or document. *Jackson was fired for repeatedly refusing to follow protocol.*

provident ('prov·i·dĕnt) *adj.* wisely providing for future needs; frugal, economical. *Because my parents were so provident, I didn't have to struggle to pay for college.*

proxy ('prok·see) *n.* 1. a person or agent authorized to represent or act for another. 2. a document authorizing this substitution. *The president appointed a proxy to handle business matters during his absence.*

prudent ('proo·dĕnt) *adj.* careful and sensible regarding one's actions and interests; exercising good judgment, judicious. *Clarissa has always been very prudent, so her recent bout of poor choices and boisterous behavior tells me she is very upset about something.*

puerile ('pyoŏ·rĭl) *adj.* 1. childish, immature. 2. suitable only for children, belonging to or of childhood. *Andrew is a remarkably successful businessman for someone so puerile.*

pugnacious (pug·'nay·shŭs) *adj.* contentious, quarrelsome, eager to fight, belligerent. *Don't be so pugnacious—I don't want to fight.*

punctilious (pungk·'til·i·ŭs) *adj.* extremely attentive to detail, very meticulous and precise. *One of the reasons he excels as an editor is because he is so punctilious.*

pundit ('pun·dit) *n.* a learned person or scholar; one who is an authority on a subject. *The journalist consulted several legal pundits before drafting the article.*

pungent ('pun·jĕnt) *adj.* 1. having a strong, sharp taste or smell. 2. penetrating, caustic, stinging. *I love the pungent taste of a good, strong curry.*

purge (purj) *v.* to free from impurities, especially to rid of that which is undesirable or harmful; to make or become clean, pure. *After Leon writes a draft, he purges the text of unnecessary words to make it more succinct.*

purloin (pŭr·'loin) *v.* to steal. *The thief purloined a sculpture worth thousands of dollars.*

purport ('pur·pohrt) *v.* 1. to be intended to seem, to have the appearance of being. 2. propose or intend. *The letter purports to express your opinion on the matter.*

Q

quaff (kwahf) *v.* to drink hurriedly or heartily; to swallow in large draughts. *He quickly quaffed three glasses of water.*

quail (kwayl) *v.* to draw back in fear, flinch, cower. *Mona quailed as soon as the vicious dog entered the room.*

querulous ('kwer·ŭ·lŭs) *adj.* complaining, peevish, discontented. *He's a cantankerous and querulous old man, but I love him.*

queue (kyoo) *n.* 1. a line of people or vehicles waiting their turn. 2. (in information processing) an ordered list of tasks to be performed or sequence of programs awaiting processing. *Look how long the queue is! We'll be waiting for hours.*

quid pro quo (kwid proh 'kwoh) *n.* a thing given in return for something; an equal exchange or substitution. *I won't agree to any deal that isn't quid pro quo— it must be a win-win arrangement.*

quiescent (kwi·'es·ĕnt) *adj.* inactive, quiet, at rest; dormant, latent. *The volcano is quiescent at the moment, but who knows when it will erupt again.*

quintessence (kwin·'tes·ĕns) *n.* 1. the essence of a substance. 2. the perfect example or embodiment of something. *Maura is the quintessence of kindness.*

quixotic (kwik·'sot·ik) *adj.* extravagantly chivalrous and unselfish; romantically idealistic, impractical. *His quixotic ways charmed all the women at the dance.*

quotidian (kwoh·'tid·ee·ăn) *adj.* 1. daily. 2. commonplace, pedestrian. *Prudence took her quotidian dose of medicine.*

R

rakish ('ray·kish) *adj*. 1. debonair, smartly dressed or mannered, jaunty in appearance or manner. 2. unconventional and disreputable; dissolute or debauched. *The rakish young woman charmed everyone at the table.*

rancor ('rang·kŏr) *n*. a bitter feeling of ill will, long-lasting resentment. *Greg is full of rancor towards his brother, and this causes tension at family gatherings.*

rapacious (ră·'pay·shŭs) *adj*. excessively greedy and grasping (especially for money); voracious, plundering. *The rapacious general ordered his soldiers to pillage the town.*

raucous ('raw·kŭs) *adj*. 1. unpleasantly loud and harsh. 2. boisterous, disorderly, disturbing the peace. *The raucous music kept us awake all night.*

reactionary (ree·'ak·shŏ·ner·ee) *n*. a person who favors political conservativism; one who is opposed to progress or liberalism. *It should be an interesting marriage: he's a reactionary and she's as liberal as they come.*

rebuke (ri·'byook) *v*. 1. to criticize sharply; to reprove or reprimand, censure. 2. to repress or restrain by expressing harsh disapproval. *After weeks of being rebuked in front of his coworkers for minor infractions and imaginary offenses, Ameer realized he was being persecuted by his boss.*

recalcitrant (ri·'kal·si·trănt) *adj*. disobedient, unruly, refusing to obey authority. *The recalcitrant child was sent to the principal's office for the third time in a week.*

recidivism (ri·'sid·ĭ·vizm) *n*. a relapse or backslide, especially into antisocial or criminal behavior after conviction and punishment. *Allowing prisoners to earn their GED or a college degree has been shown to greatly reduce recidivism.*

recondite ('rek·ŏn·dīt) *adj*. 1. not easily understood, obscure, abstruse. 2. dealing with abstruse or profound matters. *He loves the challenge of grasping a recondite subject.*

reconnoiter (ree·kŏ·'noi·tĕr) *v*. to make a preliminary inspection or survey of, especially to gather military information or prepare for military operations. *My job was to reconnoiter the party and let my friends know if it was worth attending.*

refractory (ri·'frak·tŏ·ree) *adj*. stubborn, unmanageable, resisting control or discipline. *Elena is a counselor for refractory children in an alternative school setting.*

regale (ri·'gayl) *v*. to delight or entertain with a splendid feast or pleasant amusement. *The king regaled his guests until the early morning hours.*

remonstrate (ri·'mon·strayt) *v.* 1. to say or plead in protest, objection, or opposition. 2. to scold or reprove. *The children remonstrated loudly when their mother told them they couldn't watch that movie.*

rendezvous ('rahn·dě·voo) *n.* 1. a prearranged meeting at a certain time and place. 2. a place where people meet, especially a popular gathering place. *v.* to bring or come together at a certain place, to meet at a rendezvous. *Clarissa and Ahmed planned a rendezvous in the park after lunch.*

renegade ('ren·ě·gayd) *n.* 1. a deserter; one who rejects a cause, group, etc. 2. a person who rebels and becomes an outlaw. *The renegade soldier decided to join the guerrilla fighters.*

renowned (ri·'nownd) *adj.* famous; widely known and esteemed. *The renowned historian Stephen Ambrose wrote many books that were popular both with scholars and the general public.*

repartee (rep·ăr·'tee) *n.* 1. a quick, witty reply. 2. the ability to make witty replies. *He wasn't expecting such a sharp repartee from someone who was normally so quiet.*

replete (ri·'pleet) *adj.* 1. well stocked or abundantly supplied. 2. full, gorged. *The house was replete with expensive antiques.*

repose (ri·'pohz) *n.* 1. resting or being at rest. 2. calmness, tranquility, peace of mind. *The wail of a police siren disturbed my repose.*

reprehensible (rep·ri·'hen·sĭ·běl) *adj.* deserving rebuke or censure. *The reprehensible behavior of the neighborhood bully angered everyone on the block.*

reprieve (ri·'preev) *n.* 1. postponement or cancellation of punishment, especially of the death sentence. 2. temporary relief from danger or discomfort. *The court granted him a reprieve at the last moment because of DNA evidence that absolved him.*

reprisal (ri·'prī·zăl) *n.* 1. an act of retaliation for an injury with the intent of inflicting at least as much harm in return. 2. the practice of using political or military force without actually resorting to war. *The president promised a swift reprisal for the attack.*

reprobate ('rep·rŏ·bayt) *n.* an immoral or unprincipled person; one without scruples. *Edgar deemed himself a reprobate, a criminal, and a traitor in his written confession.*

repudiate (ri·'pyoo·di·ayt) *v.* to disown, disavow, reject completely. *Mrs. Tallon has repeatedly repudiated your accusations.*

rescind (ri·'sind) *v.* to repeal or cancel; to void or annul. *The Olsens rescinded their offer to buy the house when they discovered the property was in a flood zone.*

resonant ('rez·ŏ·nănt) *adj.* echoing, resounding. *The new announcer at the stadium has a wonderfully resonant voice.*

resplendent (ri·'splen·dĕnt) *adj.* having great splendor or beauty; dazzling, brilliant. *Sanjay stood for a long time on the deck, watching a resplendent sunset over the mountains.*

reticent ('ret·i·sĕnt) *adj.* tending to keep one's thoughts and feelings to oneself; reserved, untalkative, silent. *Annette is very reticent, so don't expect her to tell you much about herself.*

revere (ri·'veer) *v.* to regard with reverence or awe; to venerate, hold in highest respect or estimation. *When you look at Judith's work, it's easy to see which painter she reveres most; every painting is an homage to Cezanne.*

rigmarole ('rig·mă·rohl) (also **rigamarole**) *n.* 1. rambling, confusing, incoherent talk. 2. a complicated, petty procedure. *We had to go through a great deal of rigmarole to get this approved.*

rogue (rohg) *n.* 1. a dishonest, unprincipled person. 2. a pleasantly mischievous person. 3. a vicious and solitary animal living apart from the herd. *Yesterday, that rogue hid all of my cooking utensils; today he's switched everything around in the cupboards!*

roil (roil) *v.* 1. to make a liquid cloudy or muddy. 2. to stir up or agitate. 3. to anger or annoy. *The crowd was roiled by the speaker's insensitive remarks.*

rubric ('roo·brik) *n.* 1. a class or category. 2. a heading, title, or note of explanation or direction. *I would put this under the rubric of "quackery," not "alternative medicine."*

S

sacrilegious (sak·rĭ·'lij·ŭs) *adj.* disrespectful or irreverent towards something regarded as sacred. *Her book was criticized by the church for being sacrilegious.*

sagacious (să·'gay·shŭs) *adj.* having or showing sound judgment; perceptive, wise. *My sagacious uncle always gives me good, sound advice.*

salient ('say·lee·ĕnt) *adj.* 1. conspicuous, prominent, highly noticeable; drawing attention through a striking quality. 2. springing up or jutting out. *Jill's most salient feature is her stunning auburn hair.*

salutary ('sal·yŭ·ter·ee) *adj.* producing a beneficial or wholesome effect; remedial. *To promote better health, I've decided to move to a more salutary climate.*

sanctimonious (sangk·tĭ·'moh·nee·ŭs) *adj.* hypocritically pious or devout; excessively self-righteous. *The thief's sanctimonious remark that "a fool and his money are soon parted" only made the jury more eager to convict him.*

sanction ('sangk·shŏn) *n.* 1. official authorization or approval. 2. a penalty imposed to coerce another to comply or conform. *v.* 1. to approve or permit; to give official authorization or approval for, ratify. *The city council has sanctioned our request to turn the empty lot into a community garden.*

sangfroid (sahn·'frwah) *n.* composure, especially in dangerous or difficult circumstances. *I wish I had Jane's sangfroid when I find myself in a confrontational situation.*

sanguine ('sang·gwin) *adj.* 1. confidently cheerful, optimistic. 2. of the color of blood; red. *People are drawn to her because of her sanguine and pleasant nature.*

sardonic (sahr·'don·ik) *adj.* sarcastic, mocking scornfully. *I was hurt by his sardonic reply.*

saturnine ('sat·ŭr·nīn) *adj.* gloomy, dark, sullen. *The saturnine child sulked for hours.*

savoir faire ('sav·wahr 'fair) *n.* knowledge of the right thing to do or say in a social situation; graceful tact. *Adele's savoir faire makes her the quintessential hostess.*

schism ('siz·ĕm) *n.* a separation or division into factions because of a difference in belief or opinion. *The schism between the two parties was forgotten as they united around a common cause.*

scintilla (sin·'til·ă) *n.* a trace or particle; minute amount, iota. *She has not one scintilla of doubt about his guilt.*

scintillating ('sin·tĭ·lay·ting) *adj.* 1. sparkling, shining brilliantly. 2. brilliantly clever and animated. *I had planned to leave the dinner party early, but the conversation was so scintillating that I stayed until 2:00 in the morning.*

scurvy ('skur·vee) *adj.* contemptible, mean. *That scurvy knave has ruined my plans again.*

seditious (si·'dish·ŭs) *adj.* arousing to insurrection or rebellion; engaging in or promoting sedition (conduct or language which incites resistance or opposition to lawful authority). *Toby's seditious behavior nearly started a riot at the town meeting.*

sedulous ('sej·ŭ·lŭs) *adj.* diligent, persevering, hard working. *After years of sedulous research, the researchers discovered a cure.*

semantics (si·'man·tiks) *n.* 1. the study of meaning in language. 2. the meaning, connotation, or interpretation of words, symbols, or other forms. 3. the study of relationships between signs or symbols and their meanings. *He claims it's an issue of semantics, but the matter is not open to interpretation.*

sententious (sen·'ten·shŭs) *adj.* 1. expressing oneself tersely, pithy. 2. full of maxims and proverbs offered in a self-righteous manner. *I was looking for your honest opinion, not a sententious reply.*

servile ('sur·vīl) *adj.* 1. pertaining to or befitting a slave or forced labor. 2. abjectly submissive, slavish. *The climax comes when Yolanda, who had believed she was doomed to play the role of a servile wife to a domineering husband, finds the courage to break the engagement and marry the man she truly loves.*

shiftless ('shift·lis) *adj.* lazy and inefficient; lacking ambition, initiative, or purpose. *My shiftless roommate has failed all of his classes.*

simian ('sim·ee·ăn) *adj.* of or like an ape or monkey. *Scientists have studied humans' simian ancestors.*

sinuous ('sin·yoo·ŭs) *adj.* winding, undulating, serpentine. *It is dangerous to drive fast on such a sinuous road.*

slake (slayk) *v.* 1. to satisfy, quench. 2. to reduce the intensity of, moderate, allay. *The deer slaked its thirst at the river.*

sodden ('sod·ĕn) *adj.* 1. thoroughly saturated, soaked. 2. expressionless or dull, unimaginative. *Caught in an unexpected rainstorm, I was sodden by the time I reached the bus stop.*

solecism ('sol·ĕ·siz·ĕm) *n.* 1. a mistake in the use of language. 2. violation of good manners or etiquette, impropriety. *Frank's solecism caused his debate team much embarrassment.*

solicit (sŏ·'lis·it) *v.* 1. to ask for earnestly, petition. 2. to seek to obtain by persuasion or formal application. 3. to approach with an offer for paid services. *Cy was touting the merits of the referendum as he solicited support for Tuesday's vote.*

sophistry ('sof·i·stree) *n.* clever but faulty reasoning; a plausible but invalid argument intended to deceive by appearing sound. *I was amused by his sophistry, but knew he had a little more research to do before he presented his argument to the distinguished scholars in his field.*

sordid ('sor·did) *adj.* 1. dirty, wretched, squalid. 2. morally degraded. *This sordid establishment should be shut down immediately.*

specious ('spee·shŭs) *adj.* 1. seemingly plausible but false. 2. deceptively pleasing in appearance. *Vinnie did not fool me with his specious argument.*

spurious ('spyoor·ee·ŭs) *adj.* false, counterfeit, not genuine or authentic. *Ian's surreptitious manner makes me believe his support for you is spurious and that he has a hidden agenda.*

squalid ('skwol·id) *adj.* 1. filthy and wretched. 2. morally repulsive, sordid. *The housing inspectors noted such deplorable and squalid living conditions in the decrepit building on Water Street that they were forced to evacuate the tenants.*

staunch (stawnch) *v.* (also **stanch**) stopping the flow of something. *adj.* firm and steadfast, unswerving; firm and constant in principle or loyalty. *I have always been a staunch believer in the power of positive thinking.*

steadfast ('sted·fast) *adj.* 1. firmly fixed or unchanging, resolute. 2. firmly loyal and constant, unswerving. *The captain held a steadfast course despite the rough seas.*

stoical ('stoh·i·kăl) *adj.* seemingly unaffected by pleasure or pain; indifferent, impassive. *Michael was stoical, but underneath, he is every bit as emotional as we are.*

strident ('strī·dĕnt) *adj.* unpleasantly loud and harsh; grating, shrill, discordant. *When he heard the strident tone of his mother's voice, Oscar knew he was in big trouble.*

stultify ('stul·tĭ·fī) *v.* 1. to impair or make ineffective, cripple. 2. to make (someone) look foolish or incompetent. *Of course I'm angry! You stultified me at that meeting!*

stymie ('stī·mee) *v.* to hinder, obstruct, thwart; to prevent the accomplishment of something. *The negotiations were stymied by yet another attack.*

sublime (sŭ·'blīm) *adj.* having noble or majestic qualities; inspiring awe, adoration, or reverence; lofty, supreme. *Beethoven's music is simply sublime.*

subliminal (sub·'lim·ĭ·năl) *adj.* below the threshold of consciousness. *Subliminal advertising is devious but effective.*

subvert (sub·'vurt) *v.* 1. to overthrow. 2. to ruin, destroy completely. 3. to undermine. *She quietly subverted his authority by sharing internal information with outside agents.*

succinct (sŭk·'singkt) *adj.* expressed clearly and precisely in few words; concise, terse. *Cole's eloquent and succinct essay on the power of positive thinking won first place in the essay contest.*

succor ('suk·ŏr) *n.* assistance or relief in time of difficulty or distress. *v.* to provide assistance or relief in time of difficulty or distress. *The Red Cross and other relief organizations provide succor to the needy during natural disasters.*

sundry ('sun·dree) *adj.* various, miscellaneous. *The sundry items in her backpack reveal a great deal about her personality.*

supercilious (soo·pĕr·'sil·ee·ŭs) *adj.* haughty, scornful, disdainful. *Sunil's supercilious attitude and sarcastic remarks annoy me greatly.*

supplicant ('sup·lĭ·kănt) *n.* a person who asks humbly for something; one who beseeches or entreats. *The supplicants begged for forgiveness.*

surfeit ('sur·fit) *n.* 1. an excessive amount or overabundance; glut. 2. the state of being or eating until excessively full. *v.* to feed or fill to excess, satiety, or disgust; overindulge. *In some countries, the leaders and a select few enjoy a surfeit of wealth while most of the population lives in squalor.*

surly ('sur·lee) *adj.* bad-tempered, gruff, or unfriendly in a way that suggests menace. *Emily received a surly greeting from the normally cheerful receptionist.*

surmise (sŭr·'mīz) *v.* to infer based upon insufficient evidence; to guess, conjecture. *After finding dirty footprints in her apartment, Lakisha surmised that someone had stolen her misplaced jewelry.*

surreptitious (sur·ĕp·'tish·ŭs) *adj.* 1. done, made, or obtained through stealthy, clandestine, or fraudulent means. 2. marked by or acting with stealth or secrecy. *Ian's surreptitious manner makes me believe his support for you is spurious and that he has a hidden agenda.*

surrogate ('sur·ŏ·git) *n.* a substitute; one who takes the place of another. *Martha agreed to be a surrogate mother for her sister.*

svelte (svelt) *adj.* slender and graceful, suave. *The svelte actress offered a toast to her guests.*

sycophant ('sik·ŏ·fănt) *n.* a person who tries to win the favor of influential or powerful people through flattery; a fawning parasite. *Omar realized that one of the drawbacks of his celebrity was that he would always be surrounded by sycophants.*

T

taciturn ('tas·i·turn) *adj.* habitually untalkative, reserved. *I've always known him to be taciturn, but yesterday he regaled me with tales of his hiking adventures.*

tangential (tan·ʹjen·shăl) *adj.* 1. only superficially relevant; of no substantive connection. 2. of or relating to a tangent. *Rudy's thesis paper contained tangential statements, not relevant facts.*

tangible (ʹtan·jĭ·bĕl) *adj.* able to be perceived by touch, palpable; real or concrete. *There is no tangible evidence of misconduct; it's all hearsay.*

tawdry (ʹtaw·dree) *adj.* gaudy or showy but without any real value; flashy and tasteless. *I've never seen such a tawdry outfit as the three-tiered taffeta prom gown that the music singer wore to the awards ceremony!*

teem (teem) *v.* to be full of; to be present in large numbers. *The fisherman found a stream teeming with bass.*

temerity (tĕ·ʹmer·i·tee) *n.* foolish disregard of danger; brashness, audacity. *This is no time for temerity; we must move cautiously to avoid any further damage.*

tenacious (tĕ·ʹnay·shŭs) *adj.* 1. holding firmly to something, such as a right or principle; persistent, stubbornly unyielding. 2. holding firmly, cohesive. 3. sticking firmly, adhesive. 4. (of memory) retentive. *When it comes to fighting for equality, she is the most tenacious person I know.*

tendentious (ten·ʹden·shŭs) *adj.* biased, not impartial, partisan; supporting a particular cause or position. *The tendentious proposal caused an uproar on the Senate floor.*

tenet (ʹten·it) *n.* a belief, opinion, doctrine or principle held to be true by a person, group, or organization. *This pamphlet describes the tenets of Amnesty International.*

tenuous (ʹten·yoo·ŭs) *adj.* 1. unsubstantial, flimsy. 2. having little substance or validity. *Though the connection between the two crimes seemed tenuous at first, a thorough investigation showed they were committed by the same person.*

terse (turs) *adj.* concise, using no unnecessary words, succinct. *After our disagreement, Heidi and I engaged only in terse exchanges.*

thwart (thwort) *v.* to prevent the accomplishment or realization of something. *The general thwarted an attack by the opposing army.*

timid (ʹtim·id) *adj.* lacking confidence, conviction, or courage; fearful, hesitant, shy. *Adele was so timid she could barely muster the courage to look another person in the eye.*

timorous (ʹtim·ŏ·rŭs) *adj.* fearful, timid, afraid. *The stray dog was timorous, and it took a great deal of coaxing to get him to come near the car.*

tirade ('tī·rayd) *n.* a long, angry, often highly critical speech; a violent denunciation or condemnation. *Since Andre was known for his temper, his tirade did not surprise his roommate.*

toil (toil) *n.* exhausting labor or effort; difficult or laborious work. *v.* to work laboriously, labor strenuously. *Evan toiled for hours before solving the problem.*

totalitarian (toh·tal·i·'tair·ee·ăn) *adj.* of a form of government in which those in control neither recognize nor tolerate rival parties or loyalties, demanding total submission of the individual to the needs of the state. *The totalitarian regime fell quickly when the people revolted.*

tout (towt) *v.* 1. to promote or praise highly and energetically, especially with the goal of getting a customer, vote, etc. 2. to solicit (customers, votes, etc.) in an especially brazen or persistent manner. *Cy was touting the merits of the referendum as he solicited support for Tuesday's vote.*

tractable ('trak·tă·běl) *adj.* easily managed or controlled; obedient, docile. *In the novel* Brave New World, *the World Controllers use hypnosis and a "happiness drug" to make everyone tractable.*

transient ('tran·zhěnt) *adj.* lasting only a very short time; fleeting, transitory, brief. *Their relationship was transient but profound.*

trenchant ('tren·chănt) *adj.* 1. penetrating, forceful, effective. 2. extremely perceptive, incisive. 3. clear-cut, sharply defined. *It was a trenchant argument, and it forced me to change my mind about the issue.*

tribunal (trī·'byoo·năl) *n.* a court of justice. *He will be sentenced for his war crimes by an international tribunal.*

trite (trīt) *adj.* repeated too often, overly familiar through overuse; worn out, hackneyed. *The theme of the novel was trite; many writers had written about death in a similar way.*

truculent ('truk·yŭ·lěnt) *adj.* 1. defiantly aggressive. 2. fierce, violent. 3. bitterly expressing opposition. *The outspoken congresswoman gave a truculent speech arguing against the proposal.*

truncate ('trung·kayt) *v.* to shorten or terminate by (or as if by) cutting the top or end off. *The glitch in the software program truncated the lines of a very important document I was typing.*

tumultuous (too·'mul·choo·ŭs) *adj.* 1. creating an uproar, disorderly, noisy. 2. a state of confusion, turbulence, or agitation, tumult. *It was another tumultuous day for the stock market, and fluctuating prices wrought havoc for investors.*

turpitude ('tur·pi·tood) *n.* 1. wickedness. 2. a corrupt or depraved act. *Such turpitude deserves the most severe punishment.*

U

umbrage ('um·brij) *n.* offense, resentment. *I took great umbrage at your suggestion that I twisted the truth.*

unctuous ('ungk·choo·ŭs) *adj.* 1. unpleasantly and excessively or insincerely earnest or ingratiating. 2. containing or having the quality of oil or ointment; greasy, slippery, suave. *I left without test driving the car because the salesperson was so unctuous that I couldn't trust him.*

undermine (un·dĕr·'mīn) *v.* 1. to weaken or injure, especially by wearing away at the foundation. 2. to destroy in an underhanded way. *By telling the children that they could eat chocolate, the babysitter undermined their mother, who had forbade them to eat sweets.*

undulate ('un·jŭ·layt) *v.* to move in waves or in a wavelike fashion, fluctuate. *The curtains undulated in the breeze.*

untoward (un·'tohrd) *adj.* 1. contrary to one's best interest or welfare; inconvenient, troublesome, adverse. 2. improper, unseemly, perverse. *Jackson's untoward remarks made Amelia very uncomfortable.*

upbraid (up·'brayd) *v.* to reprove, reproach sharply, condemn; admonish. *The child was upbraided for misbehaving during the ceremony.*

urbane (ur·'bayn) *adj.* elegant, highly refined in manners, extremely tactful and polite. *Christopher thinks he's so urbane, but he's really quite pedestrian.*

usurp (yoo·'surp) *v.* to seize, or take possession of, by force and without right; to wrongfully take over. *After the king's half-brother usurped the throne, he executed the king and queen and imprisoned the prince, who was the rightful heir to the throne.*

V

vacillate ('vas·ĭ·layt) *v.* 1. to move or sway from side to side, fluctuate. 2. to swing back and forth about an opinion, course of action, etc.; to be indecisive, waver. *Denise vacillated for weeks before she decided to accept our offer.*

vacuous ('vak·yoo·ŭs) *adj.* empty, purposeless; senseless, stupid, inane. *This TV show is yet another vacuous sitcom.*

vehement ('vee·ĕ·mĕnt) *adj.* 1. characterized by extreme intensity of emotion or forcefulness of expression or conviction. 2. marked by great force, vigor, or energy. *The senator was vehement in her denial of any wrongdoing and maintained her innocence throughout the investigation.*

venal ('vee·năl) *adj.* easily bribed or corrupted; unprincipled. *The venal judge was removed and disbarred.*

venerable ('ven·ĕ·ră·bĕl) *adj.* worthy of reverence or respect because of age, dignity, character or position. *The venerable Jimmy Carter has won the Nobel Peace Prize.*

verbose (vĕr·'bohs) *adj.* using more words than necessary; wordy, long-winded. *Her verbose letter rambled so much that it didn't seem to have a point.*

verisimilitude (ver·i·si·'mil·i·tood) *n.* the appearance of being true or real. *The movie aims for complete verisimilitude and has painstakingly recreated the details of everyday life in the 1920s.*

veritable ('ver·i·tă·bĕl) *adj.* real, true, genuine. *Einstein was a veritable genius.*

vex (veks) *v.* 1. to annoy, irritate. 2. to cause worry to. *I was completely vexed by his puerile behavior.*

vie (vī) *v.* to compete with or contend; to strive for superiority or victory. *The two scientists were vying to be the first to find concrete evidence of extraterrestrial life.*

vignette (vin·'yet) *n.* a brief description or depiction, especially a short literary sketch or scene or ornamental sketch in a book. *The film is a series of interrelated vignettes rather than one continuous narrative.*

virulent ('vir·yŭ·lĕnt) *adj.* 1. extremely poisonous, injurious or infectious. 2. bitterly hostile or hateful, acrimonious. *They say that the pen is mightier than the sword; indeed, words can be every bit as virulent as the sting of a scorpion.*

vis-à-vis (vee·ză·'vee) *adj.* 1. referring or directing attention to. 2. face to face with or opposite to. *adv.* face to face. *After a few minutes of pandemonium, the lights came back on, and Suki suddenly found herself vis-à-vis with the man of her dreams.*

vitriolic (vit·ri·'ol·ik) *adj.* savagely hostile or bitter, caustic. *Her vitriolic attack on her opponent was so hostile that it may cost her the election.*

vituperate (vī·too·pĕ·rayt) *v.* to criticize or rebuke harshly or abusively; to censure severely, berate. *After being vituperated by her boss for something that wasn't even her fault, Jin handed in her letter of resignation.*

volatile ('vol·ă·til) *adj.* 1. varying widely, inconstant, changeable, fickle. 2. unstable, explosive, likely to change suddenly or violently. 3. (in chemistry) evaporating readily. *The stock market has been so volatile lately that I have decided to invest in bonds instead.*

voluble ('vol·yŭ·běl) *adj.* 1. talking a great deal and with great ease; language marked by great fluency; rapid, nimble speech. 2. turning or rotating easily on an axis. *Your new spokesperson is very voluble and clearly comfortable speaking in front of large audiences.*

voracious (voh·'ray·shŭs) *adj.* excessively greedy, rapacious; having a great appetite for something, devouring greedily. *I have always been a voracious reader and literally consume dozens of books every month.*

W

wary ('wair·ee) *adj.* guarded, watchful, cautious. *After being swindled by the street vendor, Bridget was wary of most salespeople.*

winnow ('win·oh) *v.* 1. to separate the grain from the chaff by using the wind or other current of air to blow the chaff away. 2. to separate the good from the bad; to examine or sift through to remove undesirable elements. *We have winnowed the list of applicants down to five highly qualified candidates.*

X

xenophobia (zen·ŏ·'foh·bee·ă) *n.* a strong dislike, distrust, or fear of foreigners. *Many atrocities have been committed because of xenophobia.*

Z

zealous ('zel·ŭs) *adj.* filled with or marked by great interest or enthusiasm; eager, earnest, fervent. *Shalom was such a zealous student that he begged his teacher to assign him extra projects.*

zeitgeist ('tsīt·gīst) *n.* the spirit of the times; the general intellectual and moral outlook or attitude characteristic of a particular generation or period of time. *The revolutionary zeitgeist of the sixties and seventies is in sharp contrast to the conservative zeitgeist of the fifties.*

zenith ('zee·nith) *n.* 1. the highest point, top, peak. 2. the point in the sky directly above the observer. *She is at the zenith of her career and has won every case this year.*

APPENDIX B

Prefixes, Suffixes, and Word Roots

PREFIXES

The following table lists the most common English language prefixes, their meanings, and examples of words with each prefix.

PREFIX	MEANING	EXAMPLES
a-, an-	not, without	atypical, anarchy, amorphous
ab-, abs-	from, away, off	abnormal, abduct, abscond
ante-	prior to, in front of, before	antedate, antecedent, antebellum
ant-, anti-	opposite, opposing, against	antidote, antagonist, antipathy
bi-	two, twice	bisect, bilateral, bicameral
circum-	around, about, on all sides	circumference, circumnavigate, circumspect
co-, com-, con-	with, together, jointly	cooperate, community, consensus
contra-	against, contrary, contrasting	contradict, contraindication
counter-	contrary, opposite or opposing; complementary	counterclockwise, countermeasure, counterpart
de-	do the opposite or reverse of; remove from, reduce	deactivate, dethrone, detract
dis-	away from, apart, reversal, not	disperse, dismiss, disinterested

PREFIX	MEANING	EXAMPLES
duo-	two	duo, duet, duality
ex-	out, out of, away from	expel, exclaim, exorbitant
in- (also il-, im- ir-)	in, into, within	induct, impart, inculcate
in- (also il-, im-, ir-)	not	invariable, incessant, illicit, inept, impervious
inter-	between, among, within	intervene, interact, intermittent
intra-	within, during	intramural, intravenous
intro-	in, into, within	introvert, introduction
mal-	bad, abnormal, evil, wrong	malfunction, malpractice, malign
mis-	bad, wrong, ill; opposite or lack of	misspell, miscreant, misanthrope
mono-	one, single, alone	monologue, monogamy, monocle
multi-	many, multiple	multiple, multimillionaire, multifarious
neo-	new, recent, a new form of	neologism, neonatal, neophyte
non-	not	nonconformist, nonentity, nonchalant
over-	exceeding, surpassing, excessive	overabundance, overstimulate
poly-	many, much	polytechnic, polyglot
post-	after, subsequent, later (than), behind	postpone, postpartum, postoperative
pre-	before	precaution, precede, presage
pro-	(a) earlier, before, prior to; in front of (b) for, supporting, in behalf of (c) forward, projecting	proceed, proclivity, profess
pseudo-	false, fake	pseudonym, pseudoscience
re-	back, again	recall, reconcile, rescind
semi-	half, partly, incomplete	semiannual, semiconscious
sub-	under, beneath, below	subconscious, subdue, subjugate
super-	above, over, exceeding	superhero, superficial, supercilious
trans-	across, beyond, through	transmit, translate, translucent
tri-	three, thrice	triangle, tricycle, triumvirate
un-	not	unable, uninterested, unorthodox
uni-	one	unite, uniform, unilateral

SUFFIXES

The following table lists the most common English language suffixes, their meanings, and examples of words with each suffix.

NOUN ENDINGS

SUFFIX	MEANING	EXAMPLES
-age	(a) action or process (b) house or place of (c) state, rank	drainage, orphanage, marriage
-al	action or process	rehearsal, disposal, reversal
-an, -ian	of or relating to; a person specializing in	guardian, pediatrician, historian
-ance, -ence	action or process; state of	adolescence, benevolence, renaissance
-ancy, -ency	quality or state	agency, vacancy, latency
-ant, -ent	one that performs, promotes, or causes an action; being in a specified state or condition	disinfectant, dissident, miscreant
-ary	thing belonging to or connected with	adversary, dignitary, library
-cide	killer, killing	suicide, pesticide, homicide
-cy	action or practice; state or quality of	democracy, legitimacy, supremacy
-er, -or	one that is, does, or performs	builder, foreigner, sensor
-ion, -tion	act or process; state or condition	attraction, persecution, denunciation
-ism	act, practice, or process; state or doctrine of	criticism, anachronism, imperialism
-ist	one who (performs, makes, produces, believes, etc.)	anarchist, feminist, imperialist
-ity	quality, state, or degree	clarity, amity, veracity
-ment	action or process; result, object, means, or agent of an action or process	entertainment, embankment, amazement
-ness	state, condition, quality or degree	happiness, readiness, goodness
-ology	doctrine, theory, or science; oral or written expression	biology, theology, eulogy
-or	condition, activity	candor, valor, succor
-sis	process or action	diagnosis, dialysis, metamorphosis
-ure	act or process; office or function	exposure, legislature, censure
-y	state, condition, quality; activity or place of business	laundry, empathy, anarchy

ADJECTIVE ENDINGS

SUFFIX	MEANING	EXAMPLES
-able, -ible	capable or worthy of; tending or liable to	flammable, culpable, inscrutable
-al, -ial, -ical	having the quality of; of, relating to, or characterized by	educational, peripheral, ephemeral
-an, -ian	one who is or does; related to, characteristic of	human, American, agrarian
-ant, -ent	performing (a specific action) or being (in a specified condition)	important, incessant, preeminent
-ful	full of; having the qualities of; tending or liable to	helpful, peaceful, wistful
-ic	pertaining or relating to; having the quality of	fantastic, chronic, archaic
-ile	tending to or capable of	fragile, futile, servile
-ish	having the quality of	Swedish, bookish, squeamish
-ive	performing or tending towards (an action); having the nature of	sensitive, cooperative, pensive
-less	without, lacking; unable to act or be acted on (in a specified way)	endless, fearless, listless
-ous, -ose,	full of, having the qualities of, relating to	adventurous, glorious, egregious
-y	characterized by, full of; tending or inclined to	sleepy, cursory, desultory

VERB ENDINGS

SUFFIX	MEANING	EXAMPLES
-ate	to make, to cause to be or become	violate, tolerate, exacerbate, emanate
-en	to cause to be or have; to come to be or have	quicken, lengthen, frighten
-ify, -fy	to make, form into	beautify, electrify, rectify
-ize	to cause to be or become; to bring about	colonize, plagiarize, synchronize

WORD ROOTS

The following table lists the most common word roots, their meanings, and examples of words with those roots.

There are more than 150 roots here, but don't be intimidated by the length of this list. To learn these roots, try breaking the list down into manageable chunks of ten to 20 roots and memorize them section by section. Some of these roots many already be familiar to you—you use words with these roots every day!

ROOT	MEANING	EXAMPLES
ac, acr	sharp, bitter	acid, acute, acrimonious
act, ag	to do, to drive, to force, to lead	agent, enact, agitate
ad, al	to, toward, near	adjacent, adhere, allure
al, ali, alter	other, another	alternative, alias, alien
am	love	amiable, amity, enamor
amb	to go, to walk	ambulatory, preamble, ambush
amb, amph	both, more than one, around	ambiguous, ambivalent, amphitheater
anim	life, mind, soul, spirit	unanimous, animosity, equanimity
annui, ennui	year	annual, anniversary, perennial
anthro, andr	man, human	anthropology, android, misanthrope
apo	away	apology, apocalypse, apotheosis
apt, ept	skill, fitness, ability	adapt, adept, inept
arch, archi, archy	chief, principal, ruler	hierarchy, monarchy, anarchy
auto	self	automatic, autonomy, automaton
be	to be, to have a certain quality	befriend, bemoan, belittle
bel, bell	war	rebel, belligerent, antebellum
ben, bon	good	benefit, benevolent, bonus
cad, cid	to fall, to happen by chance	accident, coincidence, cascade
cant, cent, chant	to sing	chant, enchant, recant
cap, capit, cipit	head, headlong	capital, principal, capitulate
cap, cip, cept	to take, to get	capture, intercept, emancipate
card, cord, cour	heart	encourage, cardiac, discord
carn	flesh	carnivore, reincarnation, carnage
cast, chast	cut	caste, chastise, castigate
ced, ceed, cess	to go, to yield, to stop	exceed, concede, incessant
centr	center	central, concentric, eccentric
cern, cert, cret, crim, crit	to separate, to judge, to distinguish, to decide	ascertain, critique, discern
chron	time	chronic, chronology, synchronize

ROOT	MEANING	EXAMPLES
cis	to cut	scissors, precise, incisive
cla, clo, clu	shut, close	closet, enclose, preclude
claim, clam	to shout, to cry out	exclaim, proclaim, clamor
cli, clin	to lean toward, bend	decline, recline, proclivity
cour, cur	running, a course	recur, incursion, cursory
crat, cracy	to govern	democracy, autocracy, bureaucracy
cre, cresc, cret	to grow	creation, increase, increment
cred	to believe, to trust	incredible, credit, incredulous
cryp	hidden	crypt, cryptic, cryptography
cub, cumb	to lie down	succumb, incubate, incumbent
culp	blame	culprit, culpable, exculpate
dac, doc	to teach	doctor, indoctrinate, docile
dem	people	democracy, epidemic, pandemic
di, dia	apart, through	dialogue, diatribe, dichotomy
dic, dict, dit	to say, to tell, to use words	predict, dictionary, indict
dign	worth	dignity, indignant
dog, dox	opinion	dogma, orthodox, paradox
dol	suffer, pain	condolence, indolence, dolorous
don, dot, dow	to give	donate, endow, endow
dub	doubt	dubious, indubitable, dubiety
duc, duct	to lead	conduct, induct, conducive
dur	hard	endure, durable, obdurate
dys	faulty, abnormal	dysfunctional, dystopia, dyslexia
epi	upon	epidemic, epigram, epigraph
equ	equal, even	equation, equanimity, equivocate
err	to wander	err, error, erratic
esce	becoming	adolescent, coalesce, acquiesce
eu	good, well	euphoria, eulogy, euthanasia
fab, fam	speak	fable, famous, affable
fac, fic, fig, fait, feit, fy	to do, to make	fiction, factory, feign
fer	to bring, to carry, to bear	offer, transfer, proliferate
ferv	to boil, to bubble	fervor, fervid, effervescent
fid	faith, trust	confide, fidelity, infidel
fin	end	final, finite, affinity
flag, flam	to burn	flame, flammable, inflammatory
flect, flex	to bend	deflect, reflect, flexible
flu, flux	to flow	fluid, fluctuation, superfluous

ROOT	MEANING	EXAMPLES
fore	before	foresight, forestall, forbear
fort	chance	fortune, fortunate, fortuitous
fra, frac, frag, fring	to break	fracture, fraction, infringe
fus	to pour	infusion, diffuse
gen	birth, creation, race, kind	generous, genetics, homogenous
gn, gno	to know	ignore, recognize, incognito
grad, gress	to step	progress, aggressive, digress
grat	pleasing	grateful, gratitude, ingratiate
her, hes	to stick	cohere, adherent, inherent
(h)etero	different, other	heterosexual, heterogeneous, heterodox
(h)om	same	homogeneous, homonym
hyper	over, excessive	hyperactive, hyperextend, hyperbole
id	one's own	idiom, idiosyncrasy, ideology
ject	to throw, to throw down	eject, dejected, conjecture
join, junct	to meet, to join	joint, junction, juxtapose
jur	to swear	jury, perjury, abjure
lect, leg	to select, to choose	election, select, eclectic
lev	lift, light, rise	elevator, lever, alleviate
loc, log, loqu	word, speech	dialogue, eloquent, loquacious
luc, lum, lus	light	illustrate, lucid, luminous
lud, lus	to play	illusion, elude, allude
lug, lut, luv	to wash	lavatory, dilute, deluge
mag, maj, max	big	magnify, magnitude, magnanimous
man	hand	manual, manufacture, manifest
min	small	minute, diminish, minutiae
min	to project, to hang over	prominent, imminent, preeminent
mis, mit	to send	transmit, remit, intermittent
mon, monit	to warn	monitor, admonish, remonstrate
morph	shape	amorphous, metamorphosis, anthropomorphic
mort	death	immortal, morbid, moratorium
mut	change	mutate, immutable, permutation
nam, nom, noun, nown, nym	rule, order	economy, taxonomy, autonomy
nat, nas, nai	to be born	native, nascent, renaissance
nec, nic, noc, nox	harm, death	innocent, noxious, innocuous
nom, nym, noun, nown	name	nominate, homonym, nominal

ROOT	MEANING	EXAMPLES
nounc, nunc	to announce	announce, pronounce, denounce
nov, neo, nou	new	novice, novel, neophyte
ob, oc, of, op	toward, to, against, completely, over	object, obstruct, obsequious
omni	all	omnipresent, omnipotent, omniscient
pac, peas	peace	pacify, appease, pacifier
pan	all, everyone	panorama, pandemic, panacea
par	equal	par, disparate, parity
para	next to, beside	parallel, paragon, paradox
pas, pat, path	feeling, suffering, disease	passionate, antipathy, apathetic
pau, po, pov, pu	few, little, poor	poverty, pauper, impoverish
ped	child, education	pediatrician, encyclopedia, pedantic
ped, pod	foot	pedestrian, expedite, impede
pen, pun	to pay, to compensate	penalty, punishment, penance
pend, pens	to hang, to weigh, to pay	depend, compensate, pensive
per	completely, wrong	perplex, permeate, pervade
peri	around	perimeter, peripheral, peripatetic
pet, pit	to go, to seek, to strive	compete, petition, impetuous
phil	love	philosophy, philanthropy, bibliophile
phone	sound	telephone, homophone, cacophony
plac	to please	placid, placebo, complacent
ple	to fill	complete, deplete, plethora
plex, plic, ply	to fold, to twist, to tangle, to bend	complex, comply, implicit
pon, pos, pound	to put, to place	expose, component, juxtapose
port	to carry	import, portable, importune
prehend, prise	to take, to get, to seize	surprise, apprehend, reprisal
pro	much, for, a lot	proliferate, profuse, proselytize
prob	to prove, to test	probe, probation, reprobate
pug	to fight	repugnant, pugnacious, impugn
punc, pung, poign	to point, to prick	point, puncture, punctilious
que, quis	to seek	inquisitive, conquest, query
qui	quiet	quiet, tranquil, acquiesce
rid, ris	to laugh	riddle, ridiculous, derision
rog	to ask	interrogate, surrogate, abrogate
sacr, sanct, secr	sacred	sacred, sacrament, sanction
sal, sil, sault, sult	to leap, to jump	assault, insolent, desultory
sci	to know	conscious, science, omniscient
scribe, scrip	to write	scribble, prescribe, circumscribe
se	apart	separate, segregate, seditious

ROOT	MEANING	EXAMPLES
sec, sequ	to follow	consequence, sequel, obsequious
sed, sess, sid	to sit, to be still, to plan, to plot	subside, assiduous, dissident
sens, sent	to feel, to be aware	sense, sentiment, dissent
sol	to loosen, to free	dissolve, resolution, dissolution
spec, spic, spit	to look, to see	perspective, speculation, circumspect
sta, sti	to stand, to be in place	static, obstinate, steadfast
sua	smooth	suave, persuade, dissuade
tac, tic	to be silent	tacit, reticent, taciturn
tain, ten, tent, tin	to hold	detain, sustain, tenacious
tend, tens, tent, tenu	to stretch, to thin	extend, tension, tenuous
theo	god, religion	atheist, theology, apotheosis
tract	to drag, to pull, to draw	attract, detract, tractable
us, ut	to use	abuse, utility, usurp
ven, vent	to come, to move toward	convene, venture, intervene
ver	truth	verdict, verisimilitude, veritable
vers, vert	to turn	revert, aversion, versatile
vi	life	vivid, vigorous, vicarious
vid, vis	to see	evident, survey, visionary
voc, vok	to call	vocal, advocate, equivocate
vol	to wish	volunteer, volition, benevolence

NOTES

Special FREE Offer from LearningExpress

LearningExpress will help you succeed on the TOEFL iBT

 Go to the LearningExpress Practice Center at www.LearningExpressFreeOffer.com, an interactive online resource exclusively for LearningExpress customers.

Now that you've purchased LearningExpress's *Vocabulary for TOEFL iBT*, you have **FREE** access to:

- **Reading, listening, speaking,** and **writing practice questions** covering all of the English skills tested on the TOEFL iBT
- **Sample speaking** and **writing responses** to help you understand how the TOEFL iBT is scored
- **Immediate scoring** and **detailed answer explanations**
- A **customized diagnostic report** to benchmark your skills and focus your study

Follow the simple instructions on the scratch card in your copy of *Vocabulary for TOEFL iBT*. Use your individualized access code found on the scratch card and go to www.LearningExpressFreeOffer.com to sign in. Start practicing online for the TOEFL iBT right away!

Once you've logged on, use the spaces below to write in your access code and newly created password for easy reference:

Access Code: _____   Password: _____